# Quick and Easy
# ITALIAN COOKING

CATHERINE PAGANO FULDE AND JANETTE FULDE-PORTA

BRISTOL PUBLISHING ENTERPRISES
Hayward , California

# A nitty gritty® cookbook

Printed in the United States of America.

ISBN 1-55867-298-2

Cover design: Frank J. Paredes
Cover photography: Foodpix/Miksch
Illustrations: Caryn Leschen

# CONTENTS

# THE TIME-SAVING SECRETS OF ITALIAN COOKING

Italian cuisine continues to be America's most beloved ethnic food. In fact, national polls have shown that pizza has surpassed the hamburger as America's favorite food! Why have we embraced Italy's food with such a passion? Because the freshness, variety and purity of flavor have won our hearts.

These simple flavors are easy to produce in your own kitchen with minimal time and effort. "*Quick and Easy Italian Cooking*" shows you how.

## THE ITALIAN PANTRY

Like most people today, Italians do not have the time to devote to complicated cooking, yet they like to eat well. What is their secret? They combine fresh foods with pantry staples to produce quick and satisfying meals. A well-stocked pantry provides time-saving short cuts.

### CANS AND JARS
Broths: beef, chicken, vegetable
Beans: cannellini, garbanzo, kidney
Fish: anchovies, clams, sardines, tuna
Vegetables: artichokes, fire-roasted peppers, tomatoes

### CONDIMENTS
Extra virgin olive oil
Balsamic, red wine and white wine vinegar
Capers
Black oil-cured olives
Green brine-cured olives

1

**FROZEN**

Seafood: raw and cooked shrimp, raw scallops, raw fish fillets

Meatballs

Vegetables: peas, pre-cut specialty vegetables

**NICE TO HAVE**

Bottled clam juice

Specialty imported vegetables in oil: eggplant, artichokes

Flavored oils: truffle, lemon, basil, garlic

Herb and fruit vinegars: raspberry, tarragon, fig

Bouillon cubes, gravy bases, stock reductions

Fresh vegetables and herbs in season

**DRIED**

Garlic powder

Onion powder

Flavor cubes or concentrates: vegetable, beef, chicken, mushroom, seafood

Oregano, rosemary, thyme, fennel seeds, bay leaf, allspice, Italian seasoning

Sun-dried tomatoes

Dried mushrooms: porcini, shiitake

Pastas: spaghetti, penne, rigatoni, tortellini, small elbow, etc.

Rice: Arborio, short-grained rice, Basmati

Polenta

## MAKE-AHEAD COOKING

There is an added section in the back of this book for special make-ahead basic recipes that take a little more time to prepare and cook. Prepare, divide and freeze these foods to use later. Advance preparation is both economical and convenient for the cook who does not want to use commercial broths and sauces. In addition, creating delicious food in a warm, fragrantly scented, inviting kitchen is good for the soul.

## THE ITALIAN MEAL

The family meal has four main dishes: first course, entrée, salad and dessert. The first course may be a soup, pasta or risotto. Then comes the meat, poultry or seafood, followed by a green salad. Finally there is a simple dessert. Despite the variety, the portions are small but satisfying and are all served with a regional table wine. When entertaining, the evening meal may begin with an aperitif and simple nibbles, like roasted almonds or brined olives, and end with a digestif and an elegant purchased dessert. The recipes in "*Quick and Easy Italian Cooking*" simplify the Italian meal, emphasizing one-dish preparations with larger portions. It is always nice to finish the dinner with an herbal green salad to aid digestion and some fruit or biscotti to satisfy the craving for a sweet.

# ANTIPASTI AND STARTERS

"Antipasto" simply means "before the pasta." These dishes are designed to whet the appetite for what is to come. Choose light dry wines to serve with antipasto. Light antipasti also go well with aperitifs such as Campari, sweet or dry vermouth and gin drinks.

# CITRUS-DRESSED BLACK OLIVES

Makes 1½ cups

*The variety of flavors in this recipe makes it a great starter to a delicious meal. Use organic lemons and oranges if you can.*

½ lb. brine-cured black olives
½ cup extra virgin olive oil
2 tsp. lemon juice
2 cloves garlic, sliced
zest of 1 orange
zest of 1 lemon
1 tbs. crushed fennel seeds
1 tbs. fresh lavender flowers, optional

Mix all ingredients except lavender flowers together in a serving bowl. Cover and marinate at room temperature for 4 hours, stirring occasionally. For more intense flavor, refrigerate overnight. Sprinkle with lavender flowers before serving, if desired.

# ANTIPASTO FROM JARS

*As another easy antipasto, select a variety of vegetables preserved in oil. Jars vary in size from 8.5 to 12 ounces. Save leftovers to use as toppings for pizza or flavor boosters for pasta sauces and soups.*

1 cup sun-dried tomatoes in oil
1 cup marinated artichoke hearts, sliced
1 cup marinated eggplant slices
1 cup oil-cured black olives
1 cup roasted yellow bell
   pepper slices
2 slim loaves Italian or French
   bread, sliced

Spoon vegetables into colorful dishes and serve with bread.

# BEEF CARPACCIO WITH CAPERS

*Freeze filet mignon for 3 hours before slicing it paper thin for this elegant prelude to dinner.* **Note:** *There are health concerns with eating raw meat and raw fish.*

½ lb. filet mignon, sliced paper-thin
4 tbs. superior quality extra virgin olive oil
4 tsp. capers, rinsed and drained
4 tsp. finely chopped fresh flat-leaf parsley
zest of 1 lemon
salt and freshly ground black pepper

Divide filet slices evenly among four large serving plates. Drizzle olive oil over each portion. Top with capers, parsley and lemon zest. Provide salt and pepper at the table.

### VARIATION

Sushi-grade frozen raw salmon or halibut may be served as a carpaccio. Partially thaw and slice paper-thin. Follow the above directions but substitute orange zest for the lemon and fresh mint for the parsley.

# BASIC BRUSCHETTA

*Once a poor man's food, bruschetta is now a favorite starter in restaurants.*

12 slices Italian bread
2 cloves garlic, peeled and cut in half
salt and freshly ground black pepper to taste
¼ cup extra virgin olive oil

Heat the oven to 400°. Place bread slices on a baking sheet in oven for 10 minutes. Rub toasted bread with garlic. Sprinkle with salt and pepper. Drizzle with olive oil and serve.

# BRUSCHETTA WITH TOMATO AND OREGANO

*Dried oregano combines with fresh tomatoes in this Tuscan-style bruschetta. Serve with a light, fruity red wine.*

12 slices Italian bread
1 large clove garlic, peeled and cut in half
2 cups chopped Roma (plum) or cherry tomatoes, drained
½ cup extra virgin olive oil
2 tbs. dried oregano
salt and freshly ground black pepper to taste

Heat the oven to 400°. Place bread slices on a baking sheet in oven for 10 minutes. Rub toasted bread with garlic. Set aside.

In an attractive serving bowl, combine tomatoes, olive oil and oregano. Mix well. Fold in salt and pepper. Serve with toasted bread so guest may spoon tomato mixture onto bread slices.

# MUSHROOM BRUSCHETTA

*Enjoy the earthy flavors of cremini mushrooms and fontina cheese in this Northern Italian bruschetta. Use mozzarella or Monterey Jack cheese if fontina is not available, and white button mushrooms if you can't find cremini.*

4 thick slices Italian bread
1 large clove garlic, peeled and cut in half
1 lb. sliced cremini or brown mushrooms
4 cloves garlic, thinly sliced
1 tbs. hot red pepper flakes
2 tbs. finely chopped fresh sage, or 2 tsp. dried
3 tbs. extra virgin olive oil
salt and freshly ground black pepper
3 oz. fontina cheese, shaved with a vegetable peeler

Heat the oven to 400°. Place bread slices on a baking sheet in oven for 10 minutes. Rub toasted bread with garlic. Set aside.

Arrange mushroom slices in 1 layer on a large, microwave-safe platter, working in batches if necessary. Scatter mushrooms with garlic slices, red pepper flakes and sage. Drizzle with olive oil and microwave on full power for 1 minute, or until tender and juicy.

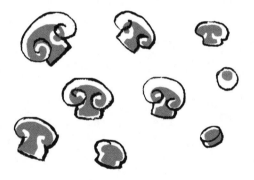

Heat broiler. Place garlic toasts on baking sheet and top with mushroom mixture and fontina shavings. Broil 5 inches from heat source until cheese melts, about 30 seconds. Serve immediately. Mushroom mixture can be prepared ahead of time and refrigerated. Let the mixture come to room temperature before assembling the bruschetta.

# PRAWNS WITH LEMON

*Lemony prawns awaken the taste buds with their tangy, refreshing flavor.*

1 lb. cooked, peeled prawns, thawed if frozen
1/4 cup lemon juice
salt and freshly ground pepper to taste
1 tbs. capers, rinsed and drained
1 tbs. chopped fresh mint leaves, or 1 tsp. dried
1/4 cup extra virgin olive oil
4 mint leaves, for garnish

In a large bowl, mix together prawns, lemon juice, salt, pepper, capers and chopped mint. Cover and marinate in the refrigerator for at least 30 minutes. When ready to serve, drain and dress with olive oil. Correct seasoning if necessary. Serve in individual bowls with mint leaves.

12    ANTIPASTI AND STARTERS

# PROSCIUTTO WITH MELON OR FIGS

Servings: 4

*This classic presentation of prosciutto di Parma is enjoyed by all ages. The sweetness of the fruit contrasts with the salty ham to satisfy our basic cravings for sweet and salty treats. Serve often when fruit is in season.*

8 wedges (2 inches thick) honeydew melon, or 8
   ripe figs, halved
8 thin slices prosciutto
lemon wedges and mint leaves, for garnish
freshly ground black pepper to taste

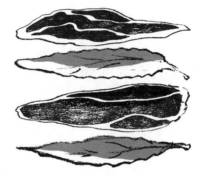

Arrange 2 melon wedges or 4 fig halves on individual serving dishes. Top each portion with 2 slices prosciutto. Garnish with lemon and mint. Provide a pepper mill at the table.

# AVOCADO WITH CHEESE
# AND BALSAMIC VINEGAR

Servings: 4

*Textures and flavors combine in this unusual antipasto. Chill cheese to make shaving easier. Serve immediately; avocado darkens when exposed to air.*

4 cups torn radicchio leaves
2 large ripe avocados, pitted, peeled and sliced
3 oz. Grana Padano or Parmesan cheese, shaved with a vegetable peeler
3 tbs. extra virgin olive oil
1 tbs. balsamic vinegar
¼ cup chopped toasted hazelnuts

Arrange radicchio and avocado slices on 4 plates. Scatter cheese shavings over avocado. In a small bowl, whisk together olive oil and balsamic vinegar and drizzle over salad. Sprinkle with hazelnuts. Serve immediately.

# GRILLED PROSCIUTTO-WRAPPED FRESH FIGS

Servings: 4

*The "secret ingredient" in this antipasto is the honey since it helps the natural sugars in the figs to caramelize. Pour a spicy red wine and enjoy the interplay of flavors.*

¼ cup honey
12 fresh black mission figs, washed and dried
6 slices prosciutto, cut in half
salt and freshly ground black pepper to taste
4 large fresh basil leaves for garnish

Prepare a medium fire in the grill. Pour honey into a shallow bowl. Dip each fig into honey, letting the excess drip back into bowl. Wrap with a half slice of prosciutto and place into a grill basket. Repeat for each fig.

Secure basket and place over fire. Grill for 2 minutes on each side, or until prosciutto is crisp. Arrange three grilled figs on each serving plate. Season with salt and several grindings of pepper. Garnish with basil leaves.

# FRIED ITALIAN CHEESE

Servings: 4

*Caciocavallo is the cheese of choice for this unusual Sicilian antipasto. If not available, use a firm provolone cheese. Caciocavallo, a mild, firm cow's milk cheese similar to provolone, is the most popular and widely used cheese in Southern Italy. Serve with a crisp white wine to emphasize the flavors.*

1/4 cup extra virgin olive oil
1 clove garlic
3/4 lb. caciocavallo or provolone cheese, cut into 1/2-inch slices
1 tbs. red wine vinegar
1 tbs. dried oregano
salt and freshly ground black pepper to taste
crusty Italian bread, sliced

In a large skillet over medium heat, warm olive oil. Add garlic and fry until fragrant and lightly browned. Remove and discard. Add cheese and quickly fry until brown on both sides, about two minutes. Sprinkle with vinegar, oregano, salt and pepper. Remove to serving plates and enjoy with bread.

# FRESH FAVA BEANS WITH PECORINO CHEESE

*The arrival of fresh fava beans to the local farmers' markets is a harbinger of spring. Select tender, bright green pods no thicker than 3/4-inch in diameter. Serve them with Pecorino Toscano (a mild, herbaceous, sheep's milk cheese, somewhat similar to Parmesan) and a glass of wine.*

3 lb. fresh young fava bean pods
1/2 lb. wedge Pecorino Toscano cheese or white Italian table cheese

Wash and dry fava bean pods. Arrange in a bundle in a rustic woven basket or serving bowl. Place cheese on a wooden board with a serving knife. Let your guests shell the beans as they eat them with slices of cheese.

# SPICY CALAMARI

Servings: 6

*Often, frozen seafood is actually fresher than "fresh" seafood because it is immediately processed and flash-frozen when it is caught. Such is the case with cleaned and sliced calamari. Look for 1-pound packages in the frozen food section of most supermarkets.*

3 tbs. extra virgin olive oil
2 cloves garlic, minced
1 tsp. hot red pepper flakes
2 pkg. (1 lb. each) frozen sliced calamari
½ cup white wine
salt and freshly ground black pepper to taste
2 tbs. chopped fresh parsley

In a deep skillet over medium heat, warm olive oil. Add garlic and red pepper flakes and cook for 30 seconds. Add frozen calamari and wine. Lower heat and simmer, uncovered for about 7 minutes, until calamari turns opaque and begins to curl. Add salt and pepper and garnish with parsley.

# OVEN-ROASTED ALMONDS

*A quick and easy treat for almond lovers.*

1 lb. raw almonds

Heat oven to 400°. Spread almonds on a foil-lined baking sheet and bake, stirring twice, until brown and aromatic, about 10 minutes.

# SOUPS

Ever wonder why Italian soups taste so good? Their hearty flavor begins with a "soffrito" sauce base, which is nothing more than an olive oil sauté of finely chopped onion, carrot and celery. Sometimes bits of prosciutto, pancetta and even smoked turkey are added for more flavor, variety and depth. As a future timesaver, sauté a large quantity of basic *Soffrito*, page 132, and freeze in quart freezer bags. Lacking a soffrito, use flavor boosters like dried beef, chicken, fish, vegetable and mushroom cubes or paste in addition to fresh and dried herbs and spices. This is where your Italian pantry staples really come in handy. Soups do not have to simmer forever to be delicious!

# RICH CHICKEN BROTH WITH TORTELLINI

*Use only premium quality ingredients for this traditional favorite.*

6 cups chicken broth
3 cloves garlic, minced
1 tbs. lemon zest
1 pkg. (9 oz.) three-cheese tortellini
1 medium head escarole, cut into bite-sized pieces (4 cups)
1 cup frozen peas
½ cup grated Parmesan cheese
lemon wedges

In a 6-quart stockpot, bring chicken broth to a boil. Add garlic, lemon zest and tortellini. Lower heat to medium-high. Cook for 5 minutes, stirring occasionally. Add escarole and peas. Continue cooking for an additional 2 minutes, until tortellini and vegetables are cooked. Ladle into bowls and top with cheese. Pass lemon wedges to squeeze over soup.

# SARDINIAN MACARONI AND BEAN SOUP

*This variation of "pasta e fagioli" uses macaroni. You can also use any small pasta shape in this filling, garlicky soup. Serve with a full-bodied wine.*

3 tbs. extra virgin olive oil
1 cup onion, finely chopped
6 cloves garlic, smashed, or 5 tbs. prepared
   garlic puree
2 cans (14 oz. each) cannellini beans,
   rinsed and drained
2 cans (14 oz. each) beef broth

1 tbs. beef bouillon base, or 1 bouillon cube
8 oz. macaroni
8 cooked *Turkey Meatballs,* page 136
1 tbs. chopped fresh rosemary, or 1 tsp.
   dried
salt and freshly ground black pepper
¼ cup grated pecorino cheese, optional

In a 6-quart stockpot, warm olive oil over medium heat. Add onion and garlic. Sauté for 5 minutes, until both are soft. Place half of the cannellini beans in a blender and puree until smooth, adding a little broth if necessary. Add puree to the pot with broth, bouillon, rosemary and remaining beans. Bring to a boil. Add pasta and meatballs. Reduce heat slightly and cook for about 10 minutes, until pasta is al dente. Season with salt and pepper and ladle into warm bowls. If desired, top with cheese.

# SICILIAN SEAFOOD SOUP

*Use prepared fish stock or bottled clam juice as a base for this flavorful soup. For a different taste, substitute 3 lb. assorted shellfish for the fish fillets.*

¼ cup extra virgin olive oil
2 cups chopped onion
4 cloves garlic, smashed
1 tsp. red pepper flakes
1 cup chopped flat-leaf parsley
1 can (14 oz.) diced tomatoes, with juice

1 cup dry white wine
1 carton (32 oz.) fish stock or clam juice
2 lb. assorted fish fillets (shark, cod, snapper, sea bass)
1 loaf crusty Italian bread

In an 8-quart stockpot, over medium heat, warm olive oil. Add onion, garlic and red pepper flakes. Sauté for 8 minutes, until fragrant. Add tomatoes, fish stock, wine, fish fillets and ½ cup of the parsley. Bring to a boil. Lower heat and simmer for 10 minutes, until fish is cooked through. Stir in remaining ½ cup parsley. Serve in warm bowls with bread.

# BUTTERNUT SQUASH AND KALE SOUP

*Scoop up spoonfuls of good health with this colorful, thick soup from Umbria featuring farro, a nutritious ancient cereal grain with a nutty flavor. Look for farro at Italian food stores. If unavailable, use instant brown rice for similar texture and flavor.*

3/4 lb. butternut squash, peeled, seeded and diced
1/4 cup extra virgin olive oil
2 large cloves garlic, minced
1 medium onion, chopped
1/4 cup chopped fresh sage
1 cup farro, washed and drained, or 2 cups instant brown rice
2 1/2 qt. vegetable broth or water, or 1 1/2 qt. liquid if using rice
1 bunch organic kale, thinly sliced
salt and freshly ground black pepper
additional olive oil for serving

Microwave squash in a covered bowl on full power for 4 minutes, until just tender. Set aside. In an 8-quart stockpot, over medium heat, warm olive oil. Add garlic, onion, sage and reserved squash. Cook for 8 minutes, until soft and fragrant. Stir in farro. Cook for 1 minute. Pour in liquid and bring to a boil. Lower heat and simmer, uncovered, for 30 minutes, until farro is tender but not mushy. Stir in kale and cook for an additional 7 minutes. Season and serve in warm bowls. Pass additional olive oil to stir into soup.

If using instant brown rice, stir in when garlic, onion, sage and squash are soft and fragrant. Pour in liquid, bring to a boil, lower heat, cover and simmer for 10 minutes, until rice is tender. Stir in kale and proceed as directed above.

# SUMMER TOMATO SOUP

*Soup in summer? Certo! Warm, room temperature, or slightly chilled, light soups are satisfying quick meals in the summer. Starchy Arborio rice is used here as a thickener instead of cream, making this lovely soup a healthy treat.*

1 small onion, finely chopped
¼ cup extra virgin olive oil, divided
½ cup Arborio rice
4 cups tomato juice
2 cups water
1 cup dry white wine
2 tbs. chopped fresh basil, or 2 tsp. dried
salt and freshly ground black pepper to taste
2 zucchini, thinly sliced
1 tbs. capers, rinsed and patted dry
fresh basil leaves for garnish, optional

In a 4-quart stockpot over medium heat, sauté onion in 2 tbs. of the olive oil until translucent. Stir in rice and coat with onion-oil mixture. Cook for 1 minute. Add tomato juice, water, wine and chopped basil. Bring to a boil, lower heat to medium-low, cover and simmer until rice is cooked, about 20 minutes. In a blender container, in batches or using a hand-held stick blender, puree soup, adding 1 tbs. of the olive oil. Season to taste with salt and pepper. Set aside to cool.

Heat remaining 1 tbs. olive oil in a small skillet over medium-high heat. Carefully add capers and fry until crisp, about 2 minutes. Remove with a slotted spoon and drain. Add zucchini to pan and quickly fry zucchini until crisp but not brown. Remove and drain. Serve the soup at room temperature garnished with some capers, a few slices of zucchini and basil leaves, if desired.

# THIRTY-MINUTE MINESTRONE

*Everyone loves minestrone! This version combines the regional flavors of Italy in one hearty dish. Add a simple green salad, some crusty bread, and dinner is ready.*

2 tbs. extra virgin olive oil
1 cup *Soffrito*, page 132, or ⅓ cup each finely chopped onion, carrot and celery
2 oz. prosciutto, chopped
1 cup Arborio rice
1 tsp. fennel seeds
2 cans (14 oz. cans) beef broth
1 qt. water
1 tsp. tomato paste
1 mushroom or beef bouillon cube

2 cans (14 oz. each) cut mixed vegetables, rinsed and drained
1 can (14 oz. each) cannellini beans, rinsed and drained
1 zucchini, diced
salt and freshly ground black pepper to taste
grated Parmesan cheese, for garnish
chopped flat-leaf parsley, for garnish
extra virgin olive oil, optional

In an 8-quart stockpot, warm olive oil over medium heat. Mix in soffrito and prosciutto. Sauté for 3 minutes, until soft. Stir in rice and fennel seeds. Stir until rice is coated and fennel seeds are fragrant.

Add broth, water, tomato paste and bouillon cube. Bring to a boil, lower heat and simmer, uncovered for 15 minutes, or until rice is cooked. Add vegetables, beans and zucchini. Cook for 5 minutes.

Season and serve with cheese, parsley and good quality extra virgin olive oil to stir in. Soup may thicken upon standing. Add a little boiling water to thin, if desired.

# PASTA AND POLENTA

Always buy 100% semolina flour pasta because of its nutty flavor and less starchy character. Cook pasta until there is only a slight resistance to the bite, "al dente." To achieve this use plenty of boiling water. Add salt, then pasta. Bring to a second boil, stirring occasionally. Start tasting when pasta is ¾ through the recommended cooking time to ensure proper texture. Drain and sauce immediately.

Fresh pasta and gnocchi should be used immediately. These soft, more delicate tasting pastas are good with cream-based sauces.

Wine is the natural companion to pasta. For everyday meals, select regional wines to complement the sauce. Soave and Orvieto are classic white wines to serve with vegetable and fish-based sauces, while Chianti, Montepulciano and Sangiovese enhance the flavor of heavier chicken and meat sauces.

The ritual of preparing polenta has intimidated many aspiring cooks, but thanks to the microwave oven, preparing creamy polenta is a snap. The robust red wines from the Piedmont area, such as Barbera, Barbaresco or Brunello, are excellent with polenta.

# BOWTIE PASTA WITH FRESH TOMATO SAUCE

Servings: 4–6

*For best tomato flavor, use home garden or farmers' market tomatoes. Add capers, olives, tuna, sardines or vegetables in oil for more substance and variety. Bowtie pasta is called Farfalle, "butterflies" in Italian.*

6 large, ripe Roma plum tomatoes, chopped
4 large fresh basil leaves, tightly rolled and thinly sliced
1 clove garlic, finely minced
3 tbs. extra virgin olive oil
1 lb. bowtie pasta (farfalle) or other pasta
½ cup grated Parmesan cheese
salt and hot red pepper flakes to taste

Place tomatoes, basil, garlic and olive oil in a large pasta bowl. Mix well and set aside for 20 minutes. Cook pasta according to package directions. Drain and add hot pasta to tomato mixture. Mix well. Add cheese and mix again. Taste and season with salt and red pepper flakes.

# SPAGHETTI WITH FRESH TOMATOES AND ARUGULA

*Spaghetti with tomatoes and arugula makes a quick, healthful side dish for grilled meats, seafood and poultry. Use baby spinach leaves if arugula is not available.*

6 large, ripe Roma (plum) tomatoes, chopped
1 large bunch arugula, washed, stemmed and patted dry

⅓ cup extra virgin olive oil
1 lb. spaghetti
1 cup grated Parmesan cheese
salt and hot red pepper flakes

In a large pasta bowl, combine tomatoes, arugula and olive oil. Mix and set aside. Cook spaghetti according to package directions. Drain and immediately add hot pasta to tomato mixture. Toss, add cheese and toss again. Season with salt and red pepper flakes and serve.

# PENNE WITH ZUCCHINI AND EGGPLANT

Servings: 4

*The color and flavor of zucchini and eggplant combine to produce an attractive, succulent topping for penne pasta.*

1 lb. penne pasta
2 large Japanese eggplants, cut into 1-inch x 3-inch strips
3 medium zucchini, cut into 1-inch x 3-inch strips
¼ cup olive oil
½ cup snipped parsley
¼ cup grated ricotta salata or crumbled feta cheese

Cook penne according to package directions. Place in a large serving bowl. Cover and keep warm.

Preheat broiler. On a foil-lined baking sheet, mix eggplant and zucchini with oil. Broil for 10 minutes until golden brown, turning after 5 minutes. Remove from oven and mix in parsley. Spoon vegetables over reserved pasta and mix well. Serve with grated ricotta salata or crumbled feta cheese.

# RAW TOMATO SAUCE TRAPANESE

*Using couscous instead of pasta brings the taste of North Africa to this favorite summertime sauce from Trapani, a town on the northwest coast of Sicily. Prepare early in the day for the best flavor.*

8 large Roma (plum) tomatoes
2 cloves garlic, minced
3/4 cup chopped fresh basil leaves
1/4 cup chopped fresh mint leaves
1 tsp. salt

1/4 cup extra virgin olive oil
1/2 cup chopped, toasted almonds
1/4 tsp. hot red pepper flakes
1 pkg. (17.6 oz.) couscous, prepared
    according to package directions

Cut tomatoes in half; remove and discard seeds. Cut flesh into 1/2-inch dice. Put into strainer to drain while preparing pesto. In a serving bowl, using a pestle or heavy spoon, mash garlic with salt. Add basil and mint, lightly crushing leaves to release fragrance. Stir in oil, almonds, red pepper flakes and drained tomatoes. Cover and keep at room temperature. When ready to serve, fluff couscous with a fork and combine with tomato sauce.

# ARUGULA PESTO WITH PENNE PASTA AND PINE NUTS

Servings: 4–6

*Peppery arugula combines with creamy pine nuts for this sophisticated variation on Genovese basil pesto. Top with avocado slices for an unusual treat.*

2 bunches (4 cups) fresh arugula, washed, stemmed and patted dry
1 clove garlic, minced
½ cup olive oil
¼ cup toasted pine nuts
½ cup grated Parmesan cheese, plus extra for topping
1 lb. penne pasta, cooked
salt and freshly ground black pepper

In a food processor workbowl, combine arugula, garlic and pine nuts. Process until well chopped. Add olive oil and process until smooth. Transfer to a large serving bowl. Stir in cheese and cooked penne. Add seasoning and serve with additional cheese.

# LARGE PASTA SHELLS WITH PEPPERS AND TUNA

Serves: 6–8

*This full-flavored dish is perfect for summertime entertaining. For best flavor, buy imported Italian tuna in oil.*

2 tbs. extra virgin olive oil
⅓ cup chopped sweet onion, such as Maui or Vidalia
1 tbs. chopped fresh flat-leaf parsley
2 cans (5½ oz. each) tuna in oil, drained and flaked, oil reserved
2 medium Roma (plum) tomatoes, seeded and chopped

3 tbs. capers, rinsed and drained
1 jar (12 oz.) roasted red peppers, drained and chopped
salt and freshly ground black pepper
½ tsp. hot red pepper flakes
1 lb. conchiglie pasta, or any shell-shaped pasta

In a large serving bowl, gently mix together olive oil, onion, parsley, tuna, ½ cup reserved tuna oil, tomatoes, capers and peppers. Season with salt, pepper and red pepper flakes. Stir well and set aside for 20 minutes for flavors to blend. Cook pasta according to package directions. Drain. Toss hot pasta with sauce. Cool for 10 minutes and serve.

# SPAGHETTINI WITH GARLIC AND OIL

*When time is short and hunger is high, do as the Italians do and throw together this simple dish in less than 15 minutes.*

1 lb. spaghettini or spaghetti
½ cup extra virgin olive oil
5 cloves garlic, chopped
1 tsp. hot red pepper flakes

2 anchovy fillets in oil, drained
½ cup minced fresh flat-leaf parsley
¼ cup toasted breadcrumbs

Cook spaghettini according to package directions. Drain, reserving 1 cup cooking water. Keep pasta warm. In a large skillet over medium-low heat, warm olive oil. Add garlic and red pepper flakes. Cook for 3 minutes, until garlic is fragrant and soft but not brown. Add anchovies. Cook briefly, mashing anchovies with a fork to dissolve them. Add parsley and ½ cup of the pasta cooking water. Simmer sauce for 4 minutes, until slightly reduced.

Raise heat and fold in reserved pasta. If too dry, add remaining ½ cup pasta water. Serve in warm bowls, sprinkled with toasted breadcrumbs.

38    PASTA AND POLENTA

# FAST LINGUINI AND CLAMS

*This is a dish that can be made in a flash. It is important to have on hand good quality canned clams, imported "pasta asciutta" (dried pasta) and fresh parsley. I use Parmesan cheese in this dish; however, many Italians do not combine seafood with cheese.*

1 lb. linguini
3 tbs. extra virgin olive oil
3 cloves garlic, crushed
1 can (10 oz.) baby clams, drained, juice
  reserved

½ cup dry white wine
2 tbs. finely chopped flat-leaf parsley
1 cup grated Parmesan cheese
hot red pepper flakes, for garnish
lemon wedges, for garnish

Cook linguini according to package directions. Set aside and keep warm. In a large skillet over medium heat, warm olive oil. Add garlic and sauté for 2 minutes, until golden and aromatic. Remove garlic and discard. Turn heat to high. Add reserved clam juice and wine. Cook for 6 minutes, whisking occasionally, until half of the liquid has evaporated and sauce thickens.

Lower heat, add clams and heat through. Fold reserved linguini into pan and coat with sauce. Add cheese and parsley. Serve with red pepper flakes and lemon wedges.

# PASTA WITH CREAMY SHRIMP SAUCE

Servings: 4

*This rich shrimp sauce may be served over farfalle, gnocchi or seafood tortellini and topped with chopped, toasted almonds, breadcrumbs or grated Parmesan cheese.*

1 lb. farfalle (bowtie pasta)
2 tbs. extra virgin olive oil, divided
1 small shallot, finely chopped
1½ lb. small raw shrimp, peeled
1 can (28 oz.) chopped tomatoes with juice

2 tbs. dry white wine
⅓ cup heavy cream
3 tbs. chopped fresh flat-leaf parsley, divided
salt and freshly ground black pepper

Cook farfalle according to package directions. Drain and keep warm. In a large skillet over medium heat, warm 1 tbs. of the olive oil. Add shallot and sauté for 3 minutes, until tender. Add remaining 1 tbs. oil and shrimp and sauté just until pink. Remove shrimp and set aside. In the same pan, add tomatoes and wine. Cook until most of the liquid has evaporated. Add cream and continue to cook until sauce thickens. Fold in reserved shrimp and heat through. Stir in reserved pasta and 2 tbs. of the parsley. Season and top with remaining 1 tbs. parsley.

# SPAGHETTI WITH CURRY

*Curry is a popular spice in Venice. The combination of curry and saffron in this dish is both spicy and mellow. It is a good accompaniment to fish entrees.*

1 lb. spaghetti
2 tbs. extra virgin olive oil
1½ tsp. curry powder
½ packet saffron
red pepper flakes to taste
1 cup light cream or 1 cup fat free milk mixed with ⅓ cup powdered non-fat milk
½ cup chopped chives

Cook spaghetti according to package directions. Drain and keep warm. In a large skillet, warm olive oil over medium heat. Stir in curry powder and saffron. Cook, stirring constantly, for 2 minutes. Add cream or enriched milk. Lower heat and simmer for 4 minutes, until sauce thickens. Add reserved spaghetti to curry sauce. Sprinkle with chives and serve in heated bowls.

# SPICY TUNA WITH CORKSCREW PASTA

*Sweet raisins balance the tangy saltiness of the tuna, and pine nuts add a surprising crunch. Fusilli, or corkscrew pasta, is perfect for catching every drop of the sauce.*

¼ cup extra virgin olive oil
¼ cup finely chopped onion
2 cloves garlic, minced
2 cans (14½ oz. each) crushed tomatoes, with juice
1 tbs. each pine nuts and raisins
¼ cup chopped fresh flat-leaf parsley, divided
2 cans (7 oz. each) imported tuna in oil, undrained
salt and freshly ground black pepper
1 lb. corkscrew pasta (fusilli)

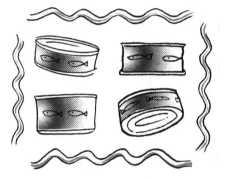

In a large skillet over medium-high heat, warm olive oil. Add onion and garlic and sauté for 3 minutes. Add tomatoes with juice. Cook for 12 minutes, until sauce has thickened. Add pine nuts, raisins and 2 tbs. of the parsley. Remove from heat. Stir in tuna with oil until well blended. Fold in pasta. Sprinkle with remaining parsley. Serve at room temperature.

# LINGUINI WITH SWORDFISH, OLIVES AND CAPERS

*This succulent dish, zesty with the flavors of sunny Sicily, is a treat for the palate as well as a feast for the eyes. Serve it with* Sicilian Citrus Salad, *page 110.*

1 lb. linguini
6 tbs. extra virgin olive oil, divided
1 lb. swordfish steaks, cut into
   1/4-inch-thick strips
12 green brine-cured olives, pitted and
   chopped
1 tbs. capers, rinsed, drained and chopped

1/3 cup fresh oregano, chopped
1/3 cup fresh mint, chopped
2/3 cup chopped fresh flat-leaf parsley
1 tsp. garlic powder
1 tsp. grated lemon zest
hot red pepper flakes to taste

Prepare linguini according to package directions; drain and set aside. In a large skillet over medium heat, warm 3 tbs. of the olive oil. Sauté swordfish strips for 2 minutes, until they begin to plump. Stir in olives, capers, oregano, mint, parsley, garlic powder and lemon zest. Cook for 4 minutes, until mixture is fragrant and begins to brown around edges. Add reserved pasta, remaining 3 tbs. oil and red pepper. Mix well and serve immediately.

# SPAGHETTINI WITH ALL THE FRUIT OF THE SEA

Servings: 4

*To prepare this pasta redolent with all the flavors of the sea, use recipe-ready frozen seafood assortments.*

1 pkg. (1 lb.) frozen mixed seafood, thawed
2 tbs. extra virgin olive oil
½ cup finely chopped green onions
1 tbs. fresh thyme leaves, or 1 tsp. dried
¼ cup chopped fresh flat-leaf parsley
¼ cup dry vermouth
1 lb. spaghettini or spaghetti
salt and freshly ground black pepper to taste

Rinse and drain seafood and set aside. In a large skillet, warm olive oil over medium-high heat. Briefly sauté onions, thyme and 2 tbs. of the parsley. Mix in reserved seafood and cook for 2 minutes. Pour in vermouth. Cook for 1 minute, until nearly evaporated. Cover and keep warm. Cook spaghettini, drain and mix with seafood sauce. Top with remaining 2 tbs. parsley.

# SEAFOOD SPAGHETTINI MARINARA-STYLE

Servings: 4

*This variation on* Spaghettini With All the Fruit of the Sea, *page 44, satisfies the red sauce lover.*

1 pkg. (1 lb.) mixed frozen seafood, thawed
2 tbs. extra virgin olive oil
2 cloves garlic, minced
3 cups prepared marinara sauce
¼ cup bottled clam juice
¾ lb. spaghettini or spaghetti

Rinse and drain seafood and set aside. In a large skillet over medium-high heat, warm olive oil. Sauté garlic for 2 minutes, until fragrant. Stir in marinara sauce and clam juice. Cook for 1 minute. Stir in reserved seafood and cook for 3 minutes until nearly cooked through. Cover, turn heat to lowest setting, and keep warm. Seafood will continue to cook, so do not overcook initially. Prepare pasta according to package directions. Drain and quickly mix with seafood sauce. Serve immediately.

# PASTA BOLOGNESE

Servings: 6

*The original Bolognese sauce uses a beef roast and hours of simmering; this classic-tasting Bolognese dresses the pasta in less than 30 minutes, thanks to the Italian method of cooking the meat in milk.*

½ oz. dried porcini mushrooms
1 cup water, divided
2 tbs. unsalted butter
3 oz. prosciutto, finely chopped
1⅔ cups *Soffrito*, page 132, or 1 cup finely chopped onion and ⅓ cup each finely
   chopped carrot and celery
1½ lb. ground chuck
1½ cups whole milk
⅓ cup tomato paste
1 beef bouillon cube, or 1 tbs. beef glace
1 lb. fresh tagliatelle or linguine pasta
grated Parmesan cheese, for garnish

Soak mushrooms in ½ cup of the water for 15 minutes, until soft. Strain through a paper coffee filter and reserve soaking liquid.

Chop mushrooms and set aside. In a large skillet, over medium-high heat, melt butter. Add prosciutto and brown for 2 minutes. Add soffrito and reserved mushrooms. Cook for 4 minutes, until soft. Quickly add meat, breaking it into small pieces with a wooden spoon. Pour in milk and continue to break up meat. Lower heat to medium and cook, uncovered, stirring occasionally, for 15 minutes, or until most of the liquid has evaporated. Stir in tomato paste, bouillon cube, reserved mushroom liquid and remaining ½ cup water. Cook for an additional 12 minutes, until sauce thickens.

While sauce is cooking, prepare tagliatelle according to package directions. Drain and toss with sauce. Serve with Parmesan cheese.

# PASTA IN PARCHMENT

*Ever wonder what to do with leftover pasta? Bake it in parchment paper or foil. Add garden produce, pantry staples, and/or herbs and spices for variety and flavor.*

½ lb. cooked pasta
2 tbs. extra virgin olive oil
3 cloves garlic, minced
½ cup chopped mixed fresh herbs (basil,
   marjoram, tarragon, parsley, chives, mint)

salt and freshly ground black pepper
1 tbs. grated lemon zest
¾ cup grated Parmesan cheese
½ cup coarsely chopped roasted pistachio
   nuts

Heat the oven to 350°. Place pasta in a colander. Run under hot water until warm and set aside. In a large skillet over medium heat, warm olive oil. Cook garlic for 4 minutes, until soft. Stir in herbs, salt, pepper and lemon zest. Add pasta and cheese. Mix well.

Cut six 15-inch squares of parchment paper or foil, fold in half, open and lie flat. Divide pasta mixture among the sheets, placing on 1 side of the crease. Top with a portion of nuts. Fold paper over filling and roll edges to make a well-sealed crescent-shaped bundle. Place on baking sheet and bake until hot, about 15 minutes. Place a packet on each dinner plate, slit and serve.

48    PASTA AND POLENTA

# PASTA SHELLS WITH CHICKEN AND GREEN OLIVES

*This is a quick chicken pasta for a fast weeknight supper. Just add a mixed green salad.*

1 lb. orecchiette pasta, or any small shell pasta

3 tbs. extra virgin olive oil

3 cloves garlic, crushed

1 can (5 oz.) whole green pitted olives, drained

2 boneless, skinless chicken breasts, cut into cubes

3 Roma (plum) tomatoes, chopped

1 tsp. dried oregano

¼ cup dry white wine

salt and hot red pepper flakes

Cook pasta according to package directions. Set aside and keep warm. In a large skillet over medium heat, warm olive oil. Add garlic and olives. Sauté for 2 minutes, smashing olives into large chunks. Add chicken pieces and sauté for 5 minutes, until chicken is brown and cooked through. Remove chicken, garlic and olives and set aside. In the same pan, add tomatoes, oregano and wine. Raise heat to high and cook for 6 to 8 minutes, until sauce is thick. Fold in reserved chicken mixture and heat through. Add pasta, toss, season with salt and red pepper flakes and serve immediately.

# LASAGNA WITH BÉCHAMEL SAUCE

*Béchamel sauce gives Northern Italian lasagna its characteristic rich flavor. This is an easy recipe for béchamel, but if time is short, use a commercially prepared Alfredo sauce.*

3 tbs. butter
1 tbs. finely chopped shallots
¼ cup flour
2 cups whole milk
salt and white pepper to taste

olive oil spray
1 pkg. (13 oz.) fresh lasagna sheets
1 jar (26 oz.) chunky marinara sauce
1 tsp. extra virgin olive oil
1 cup grated Parmesan cheese

Heat oven to 350°. In a medium skillet over medium heat, melt butter. Add shallots and sauté until soft. Stir in flour and whisk until a thick paste forms. Add milk gradually; continue to whisk until sauce is as thick as heavy cream. Season with salt and pepper. Set aside.

Spray a 9 x 13 x 2-inch baking pan with olive oil. Assemble the lasagna by placing 1 layer of pasta sheets into the pan. Spread pasta with 2 cups of the marinara sauce, then with 1 cup of the béchamel sauce. Cover with a layer of pasta. Continue layering until all ingredients are used and the last layer is béchamel. Cover the top layer with cheese and bake for 45 minutes. Cool for 10 minutes before cutting and serving.

# BAKED TRICOLOR ELBOW PASTA WITH 4 CHEESES

Servings: 6

*What an easy way to prepare Italian style macaroni and cheese!*

1 lb. tricolor elbow pasta
6 tbs. (¾ stick) butter, softened
½ cup diced fontina cheese
½ cup diced provolone cheese
½ cup diced mozzarella cheese
1 cup grated Parmesan cheese
salt and pepper to taste

Preheat oven to 400°. Prepare pasta according to package directions. Drain and remove to a large, oven-safe serving dish. Fold in butter and cheeses, mixing well. Place in oven and bake until cheeses are melted and beginning to brown, about 5 minutes. Serve.

**VARIATION**

For more adult tastes, sprinkle pasta with 1 tbs. white truffle oil and top with ¼ cup chopped, toasted almonds before serving.

# GNOCCHI WITH ASPARAGUS

Servings: 4

*Fresh asparagus and lemon zest brighten the flavor of gnocchi. Gnocchi are small pasta shapes made with potatoes mixed with flour in the dough.*

1½ lb. asparagus spears, tough ends
  removed
2 tbs. chopped shallots
¼ cup extra virgin olive oil

¼ cup chopped fresh basil, or 4 tsp. dried
1 lb. gnocchi
½ cup grated Parmesan cheese
2 tbs. grated lemon zest

In a 5-quart stockpot, bring 4 quarts water to a boil. Add asparagus spears and bring to a boil. Immediately remove blanched asparagus to a bowl of ice water to stop further cooking; save cooking water. Cut asparagus into 2-inch pieces, reserve a few tips for garnish and set both aside. In a large, microwave-safe bowl, combine shallots with olive oil and basil. Microwave, uncovered on full power for 1 minute. Stir in asparagus pieces and set aside.

Cook gnocchi in reserved asparagus cooking water for 2 minutes. Using a slotted spoon, remove gnocchi to bowl with asparagus mixture. Add cheese and lemon zest. Mix well, coating gnocchi with sauce. Add a little cooking water if sauce is too dry. Microwave, uncovered for 1 minute. Garnish with asparagus tips and serve immediately.

# SHELL PASTA WITH BROILED VEGETABLES

Servings: 6

*When using cut vegetables, indoor grilling is easiest. Use a ridged grilling pan or, for faster cleanup, cook under the broiler in a foil-lined baking sheet.*

3/4 lb. medium shell pasta
2 medium zucchini, cut into 1/2-inch coins
1 small eggplant, cut into small pieces
6 large white mushrooms, sliced
16 cherry tomatoes, halved

2 tbs. chili oil
1 tsp. garlic powder
1 cup grated Parmesan cheese
1 cup basil leaves, tightly rolled and thinly
   sliced

Prepare pasta according to package directions. Keep warm in a serving bowl. Heat broiler. On a foil-lined baking sheet, coat vegetables with chili oil. Sprinkle with garlic powder. Broil for 5 minutes. Stir and continue to broil until tender and brown around the edges, about 5 minutes. Add to reserved pasta. Stir in cheese and top with basil.

# SAUSAGE-FILLED POLENTA SLICES
# WITH MUSHROOM SAUCE

Servings: 8

*Based on an old Sicilian family recipe, this robust peasant dish becomes a quick and easy dinner by using semi-prepared ingredients and modern appliances.*

1 recipe *Creamy Polenta 1-2-3,* page 56
¼ cup extra virgin olive oil, divided
5 tbs. chopped garlic, divided
10 oz. Italian hot sausage, chopped
1 tbs. fennel seeds
2 tbs. butter, softened
1 tbs. chopped fresh rosemary, or 1 tsp. dried
1 tbs. chopped fresh thyme, or 1 tsp. dried
1 can (8 oz.) tomato sauce
1 pkg. (14 oz.) frozen sliced mushrooms
1 mushroom or beef bouillon cube

Prepare polenta. Cover and set aside. In a large skillet over medium heat, warm 2 tbs. of the olive oil. Add 3 tbs. of the garlic and cook until soft and golden, 3 minutes. Add sausage and fennel seeds. Brown over medium-high heat. Add ½ cup water. Lower heat, cover and simmer until water evaporates and sausage is no longer pink, about 5 minutes. Spoon half of the reserved polenta into a buttered 9 x 5 x 3-inch loaf pan. Arrange sausage over polenta. Spoon remaining polenta over sausage, covering it completely. Spread polenta with remaining 1 tbs. butter. Set aside and keep warm.

In the same skillet, warm remaining 2 tbs. olive oil. Add remaining 2 tbs. garlic, rosemary and thyme. Cook over medium heat for 3 minutes. Add tomato sauce, mushrooms and mushroom cube. Bring to a boil, stirring occasionally. Lower heat and simmer until sauce is thick. Pour into a serving bowl. Slice polenta. Pass at the table with mushroom sauce as a topping.

# CREAMY POLENTA 1-2-3

*This creamy dish is a wonderful addition to any meal.*

4 cups water
1¼ cups polenta or yellow cornmeal
2 tsp. salt
¼ cup (½ stick) butter
freshly ground black pepper to taste
½ cup grated Parmesan or crumbled Gorgonzola
    cheese, optional

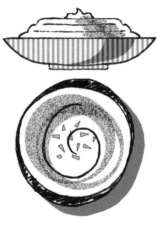

   In a large microwave-safe bowl, combine water,
polenta and salt. Cook, uncovered on full power for
12 minutes, stirring once. Remove from microwave.
Stir in butter, pepper and, if using, cheese.

# RICE AND RISOTTO

Depending upon the preparation method and type of rice, rice in Italy is either "risotto" or "riso." Risotto is made with short-grain, starchy Arborio rice, sautéed with a flavorful "sof-frito" (finely chopped onions and vegetables.) It is then coaxed to soften by gradually adding liquid which produces the creamy al dente texture. Riso is prepared very much like pasta: that is, boiled in abundant salt water until tender, drained and tossed with butter or herbs. Select light, fruity or herbaceous wines, like Rosato, Frascati or Sauvignon Blanc.

# SEAFOOD RISOTTO WITH SAFFRON

*To make this fast dish, buy recipe-ready frozen seafood assortments in your supermarket or at specialty food stores.*

6 cups fish broth or chicken broth
1 tsp. butter
2 tbs. extra virgin olive oil, divided
1 chopped shallot
1 package (16 oz.) frozen mixed seafood, thawed, rinsed and patted dry
½ tsp. powdered saffron
2 cups Arborio rice
¾ cup dry white wine
⅓ cup grated Parmesan cheese
2 tbs. chopped fresh flat-leaf parsley
salt and freshly ground black pepper to taste
lemon wedges

In a small saucepan, bring broth to a simmer and keep hot. In a large skillet, over medium-low heat, melt butter with 1 tbs. of the olive oil. Add shallot and sauté for 3 minutes, until tender. Raise heat to medium-high and add seafood. Sauté for 3 minutes, or until cooked through. Remove with a slotted spoon and set aside.

In the same pan, add remaining 1 tbs. olive oil, saffron and rice. Coat rice with olive oil mixture. Add wine and cook, stirring, for 1 minute, or until alcohol evaporates.

Lower heat to medium-low. Add 1 cup of simmering broth. Stir constantly with a wooden spoon, loosening rice from bottom and sides of pan. When broth has been absorbed, add another cup. Continue stirring and adding broth as it is absorbed for about 20 minutes or until rice becomes tender and creamy. Add reserved seafood and heat through. Stir in cheese, parsley, salt and pepper. Garnish with lemon wedges and serve immediately.

# BROWN RICE AND
# WINTER VEGETABLE RISOTTO

Servings: 6

*This is a nourishing risotto for a cold day in fall or winter. Save time on cooking day by preparing the winter vegetables ahead and refrigerating them in airtight bags. Serve the risotto as a main course accompanied by steamed broccoli or cauliflower florets or as a first course to a roasted pork or turkey dinner.*

1 large clove garlic, minced
2 cups peeled, seeded, cubed butternut
  squash
1 cup cubed carrots
½ cup peeled, cubed rutabaga
3 tbs. extra virgin olive oil, divided
4 cups vegetable broth
1 tbs. unsalted butter
2 cups quartered brown mushrooms

1 small onion, chopped
1 cup Arborio rice
½ cup short-grain brown rice
½ cup dry white wine
1 cup torn baby spinach leaves
½ cup grated Parmesan cheese
salt and freshly grated black pepper to
  taste

Heat oven to 450°. In a large plastic bag, toss garlic, squash, carrots and rutabaga with 2 tbs. of the olive oil, coating vegetables with oil. Place vegetables in 1 layer on a foil-lined baking sheet and roast until tender, about 12 to 15 minutes. Remove from oven and set aside. (Or refrigerate in an airtight bag if preparing in advance. Bring refrigerated roasted vegetables to room temperature when ready to cook.)

In a small saucepan, bring broth to a simmer and keep hot. In a large, nonstick skillet over medium heat, melt butter. Add mushrooms and cook, stirring constantly, for 5 minutes, until tender. Remove to bowl. In the same pan, warm remaining 1 tbs. olive oil. Add onion and sauté until translucent. Stir in Arborio and brown rice and coat with olive oil-onion mixture. Pour in wine. Cook for about 2 minutes, until alcohol evaporates. Add 1 cup hot broth to rice mixture and stir constantly until broth is absorbed. Continue to cook, stirring and adding small quantities of broth whenever there is no more liquid in the pan. Stir and cook for 25 to 30 minutes, until rice is al dente and creamy. Add roasted vegetables, reserved mushrooms and spinach. Stir and heat through. Fold in cheese and season with salt and pepper.

# SPINACH RISOTTO WITH TOASTED PINE NUTS

Servings: 4

*Toasted pine nuts give this risotto a distinctive flavor. Briefly toast nuts in a dry skillet over medium-high heat or in a 400° oven. Watch carefully: they burn easily.*

6 cups vegetable broth
3 tbs. extra virgin olive oil
1 small yellow onion, chopped
1 pkg. (10 oz.) frozen spinach, thawed and
   squeezed dry

2 cups Arborio rice
½ cup dry white wine
1 cup grated Parmesan cheese
1 cup fresh baby spinach leaves, torn
2 tbs. toasted pine nuts

In a small saucepan, heat broth to a simmer and keep hot. In a medium skillet over medium heat, warm olive oil. Add onions and sauté for about 3 minutes, until tender. Add spinach and continue to sauté until coated with olive oil. Add rice and sauté for 1 minute. Raise heat to medium-high, add wine and stir constantly for 1 minute, until alcohol evaporates. Reduce heat to simmer. Add 1 cup of the hot broth to rice mixture and stir constantly until liquid is absorbed. Continue adding broth, about 1 cup at a time, until rice is tender and creamy. Stir in cheese and baby spinach. Set aside for 4 minutes. Top with pine nuts and serve.

# MUSHROOM RISOTTO

*Good-quality mushroom broth makes this risotto flavorful. Use porcini mushroom broth if possible.*

6 cups porcini mushroom broth (use 6 mushroom broth cubes and 6 cups water), or beef broth
3 tbs. extra virgin olive oil
1 small yellow onion, chopped
8 oz. white mushrooms, sliced

8 oz. assorted wild mushrooms, sliced
2 cups Arborio rice
½ cup dry white wine
1 cup grated Parmesan cheese
2 tbs. chopped fresh flat-leaf parsley

In a medium saucepan, heat broth to a simmer and keep hot. In a large skillet, over medium heat, warm olive oil. Add onion and sauté for 3 minutes or until tender. Add mushrooms and continue to sauté until coated with olive oil. Stir in rice and sauté for 1 minute. Raise heat and add wine, stirring until alcohol evaporates. Lower heat to simmer. Add 1 cup of the hot broth to rice mixture, stirring constantly until liquid is absorbed. Continue adding broth and stirring for 20 to 25 minutes until rice is tender and creamy. Add cheese and parsley. Set aside for 3 minutes and serve immediately.

# ORANGE RISOTTO IN PARMESAN CHEESE CUPS

Servings: 4

*Adriana Migliorini, a creative hostess from Adria, Italy, inspired this recipe. She serves this risotto in Parmesan cheese cups as an elegant first course.*

4 cups vegetable broth
3 tbs. extra virgin olive oil
½ cup chopped leeks (white part only)
1½ cups Arborio rice
½ cup dry white wine
¼ cup orange juice
½ cup orange pulp (chopped orange segments)
1 cup grated Parmesan cheese
1 dash orange blossom water, or 1 pinch grated orange zest
2 tbs. chopped fresh flat-leaf parsley

In a small saucepan, heat broth to a simmer and keep hot. In a medium skillet, heat olive oil and sauté leeks for 3 minutes, until tender. Add rice and continue to sauté for 1 minute, until well coated with olive oil. Raise heat and add wine, stirring until alcohol evaporates. Lower heat and add 1 cup of the simmering broth. Stir constantly with a wooden spoon, loosening rice from the bottom and sides of the pan. When broth has been completely absorbed, add another cup, continuing to stir. Repeat this process for 20 minutes, until mixture has thickened and rice is tender. Turn off heat. Add orange juice and pulp. Stir until absorbed. Stir in cheese, orange blossom water or orange zest and parsley. Set aside for 3 minutes before serving. Serve in Parmesan cheese cups.

## PARMESAN CHEESE CUPS
3 cups grated Parmesan cheese
4 empty custard cups

On a working surface, invert custard cups. Warm an 8-inch nonstick skillet over medium heat. Sprinkle ¾ cup cheese into skillet. Warm cheese until it melts and flows together. Remove from heat. Very carefully remove cheese from pan and place over custard cups. Press down. A cheese cup will form as cheese cools. Makes 4 cheese cups.

# HERBED RICE WITH ALMONDS

*The subtle herbal flavors and crunch of roasted almonds make this buttery rice dish a favorite with children.*

4 quarts water
1 tbs. salt
1 cup Arborio rice
2 tbs. unsalted butter
2 tbs. chopped fresh herbs (parsley, sage, marjoram, mint)
2 tbs. chopped roasted almonds

In a 6-quart stockpot, bring water to a boil. Stir in salt. Add rice, bring to a second boil and cook over high heat for 10 minutes, until cooked. Drain and toss immediately with butter and herbs. Top with almonds and serve.

# BEEF, VEAL AND LAMB

The quickest and easiest ways to prepare meat are grilling, roasting and sautéing. Our recipes represent simple, home cooking of veal, lamb, and beef.

# VEAL SCALLOPINI WITH BALSAMIC GLAZE

*Balsamic vinegar cuts the sweetness of the Marsala wine in this traditional dish. Pour a robust wine to underscore the complex flavors of this entrée.*

1½ lb. veal scallopini, pounded to ¼-inch
   thickness
½ cup flour
garlic powder
¼ cup olive oil

1 cup Marsala wine
1 cup chicken broth
2 tbs. balsamic vinegar
2 tbs. finely chopped parsley

Dust veal scallopini with flour. Sprinkle with garlic powder. In a large skillet, warm olive oil over medium-high heat. Brown scallopini in batches for 2 minutes on each side. Transfer to a platter. Pour off fat from skillet. Add Marsala and chicken broth. Boil over high heat for 2 minutes, scraping brown bits from bottom of pan. Lower heat, add balsamic vinegar and return veal to pan. Cover and simmer over low heat for 8 minutes.

Remove scallopini to serving dish and keep warm. Turn heat to high and reduce sauce, whisking constantly for 1 minute until syrupy. Pour sauce over scallops, garnish with parsley and serve.

# LAMB STEAKS WITH MUSTARD AND WALNUTS

Servings: 6–8

*Ask your butcher to cut a boneless lamb leg into steaks for this party dish. the walnuts are a surprising crunchy touch.*

8 lamb steaks, cut ¾-inch thick
garlic powder
freshly ground black pepper
3 tbs. chopped fresh tarragon, or 3 tsp. dried
3 tbs. extra virgin olive oil

3 shallots, chopped
1 cup zinfandel or other red wine
3 tbs. whole grain mustard
½ cup meat broth (use lamb bouillon and water) or beef broth
⅓ cup chopped toasted walnuts

Prepare lamb steaks by sprinkling each side with garlic powder, pepper and tarragon. In a large skillet, over medium-high heat, warm olive oil. Cook lamb for 3 minutes on each side, until brown. Remove and keep warm. Lower heat to medium and sauté shallots for 3 minutes. Whisk in wine, mustard and meat broth. Raise heat and cook for 3 minutes until sauce thickens. Lower heat, return lamb to skillet and turn over to coat with sauce. Simmer for 1 minute, until heated through. Serve with sauce and top with walnuts.

# BRACIOLINI (BEEF ROLLS)

*Thin slices of beef are spread with a breadcrumb mixture, rolled, double skewered and broiled or grilled. Quick and delicious! Pecorino Romano is a hard cheese with a stronger flavor than Parmesan. Pour a Sicilian Corvo or a Southern Italian red wine.*

1½ cups seasoned breadcrumbs
4 cloves garlic, finely minced
¼ cup finely chopped fresh flat-leaf
   parsley
¾ cup grated Pecorino Romano or
   Parmesan cheese

¼ cup extra virgin olive oil
2 oz. mozzarella cheese, sliced into thin
   discs
3 lb. thin minute steak or beef roast, sliced
   into ¼-inch-thick slices

In a medium bowl, combine breadcrumbs, garlic, parsley, Pecorino Romano and olive oil. Mix well. On a work surface, cut each meat slice into a 4 x 5-inch rectangle. Spread with 3 tsp. filling and top with 1 or 2 cheese discs. Starting at a short end, roll "jelly-roll" fashion, enclosing filling. Double skewer, securing flap. Continue until all rolls are formed. Heat broiler. Line a large baking sheet with foil. Place cake-cooling rack over foil. Place braciolini on rack about 4 inches from heat source. Broil for 3 to 4 minutes, turning once.

# GRILLED STEAK WITH PORTOBELLO AND ARUGULA TOPPING

*Italians like to serve grilled meats with flavorful toppings. Large meaty portobello mushrooms add a mellow touch to the spicy arugula for great depth of flavor.*

1 portobello mushroom
4 cups packed arugula leaves
3 cloves garlic, minced
½ cup olive oil
salt and ground black pepper to taste
4 New York strip steaks

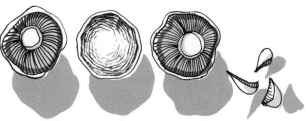

Prepare grill. Grill portobello mushroom for 5 minutes each side. Place mushroom, arugula and garlic in a food processor workbowl and chop coarsely. Place mixture in a serving bowl and stir in olive oil, salt and pepper.

Salt and pepper steaks and grill to preferred doneness. Serve steaks with topping.

# BEEF MILANESE

Servings: 4

*This recipe, associated with the Northern Italian city of Milan, is one of the most popular ways to prepare a fast meat dish in Italy. A great dish for summer, when tomatoes are at their best and fresh basil is abundant.*

4 large ¼-inch-thick slices beef or veal
2 cups milk
4 Roma (plum) tomatoes
5 fresh basil leaves
2 tbs. extra virgin olive oil
1 pinch salt
1 pinch sugar
4 cups breadcrumbs
2 eggs
2 tbs. finely grated Parmesan cheese
½ tsp. salt
¼ cup olive or vegetable oil, divided

Place meat in a bowl, cover with milk and refrigerate for 1 hour.

Cut tomatoes in half, remove seeds, finely chop flesh and place in serving bowl. Clean basil leaves and stack 1 on top of the other. Cut basil into very thin strips; add to tomatoes. Add extra virgin olive oil, salt and sugar. Mix and set aside to marinate for about 20 minutes.

In a separate shallow bowl, beat eggs and set aside. Place breadcrumbs, Parmesan cheese and salt in a large locking plastic bag. Remove 1 slice of meat from milk. Dip in egg and coat with breadcrumbs. Press to make breadcrumbs adhere and place on a large platter. Repeat this process with each piece of meat, keeping them separated on platter.

In a large skillet over medium heat, warm 1 tbs. of the olive oil. Cook each slice of beef for 2 minutes on each side, until brown. Place cooked beef on a platter and keep warm in a 200° oven until ready to serve. Repeat process until all of the beef is cooked. Serve with tomato salsa.

# POULTRY AND SEAFOOD

With an eye toward health, many Italian dishes traditionally made with red meats are now being made with turkey or chicken breasts.

Italy's geography provides such easy access to the fruit of the sea that fish and shellfish are often chosen for quick dinners. Following are some seafood presentations that we chose because of their very Italian flavors.

# CHICKEN BREASTS WITH PROSCIUTTO AND SAGE

Servings: 4

*Madeira wine adds a nutty flavor to this delicate entrée. Serve with brown rice steamed with a few sage leaves and topped with toasted slivered almonds.*

4 chicken breasts, cut in half and pounded ¼-inch thick
salt and freshly ground black pepper to taste
8 thin slices prosciutto

16 fresh sage leaves
¼ cup extra virgin olive oil
2 cloves garlic, minced
1 cup Madeira wine
1 cup chicken broth

Season both sides of chicken pieces with salt and pepper. Cover each piece with 1 slice of prosciutto and two sage leaves. Fold chicken over, enclosing both. Continue until all pieces are filled. Warm olive oil in a large skillet over medium-high heat. Sauté garlic and sage until fragrant and golden brown, about 1 minute. Add chicken, in batches if necessary, and brown for 3 minutes on each side. Remove chicken from skillet and set aside. Quickly pour in Madeira and reduce by half, whisking constantly. Add chicken broth and whisk until blended with the wine reduction. Return chicken to skillet and reduce heat to medium-low. Cover and simmer for 10 minutes, until chicken is cooked through and flavors blend.

# HERB-ROASTED CHICKEN THIGHS

Servings: 4–6

*Briefly microwaving the chicken thighs before roasting shortens cooking time for this herbaceous entrée. A Sauvignon Blanc highlights the lemony-herb flavors in this dish. Substitute parsley and basil if fresh sage and lavender aren't available.*

8 thin green onions, white and tender green parts, chopped
2 each large sprigs fresh sage, thyme, lavender and fennel
1 tbs. lemon zest
¼ cup olive oil, divided
8 skinless chicken thighs
1 tsp. garlic powder
salt and ground black pepper
   to taste
1 cup Sauvignon Blanc or
   other dry white wine
additional fresh herbs and
   lemon wedges for garnish

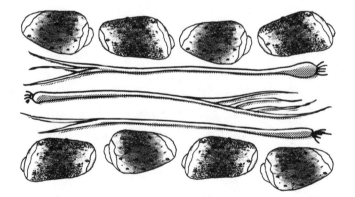

Heat oven to 400°. In a food processor workbowl or by hand with a sharp knife, mince together green onions and leaves from sage, thyme, lavender, fennel and lemon zest. Transfer onto a shallow plate.

Spread 2 tbs. of the olive oil in a 7 x 10-inch glass or ceramic baking pan. Season chicken with garlic powder, salt and pepper. Roll thighs in herbal mixture and arrange in prepared pan, bone side down.

Pour wine around chicken. Microwave, covered, on full power for 5 minutes or until chicken begins to cook. Transfer to a conventional oven. Bake, covered, until an instant-read thermometer registers 150°, about 20 minutes. Remove cover and spoon remaining 2 tbs. oil over chicken. Bake until thighs are brown and slightly crusty, about 10 minutes. Do not overcook. Garnish with herbs and lemon wedges.

# TURKEY SCALLOPINI MARSALA

*Heart-healthy turkey replaces veal in this traditional dish that freezes well. To prepare in advance, use the baking method described below. To cook and serve immediately, use either method. The richness of the scallopini requires a big, flavorful wine.*

8 turkey breast cutlets, about 2 lb.
½ cup extra virgin olive oil, divided
1½ lb. sliced white mushrooms
4 tsp. garlic powder, divided

salt and white pepper
½ cup flour
1 cup Marsala wine
2 cups beef broth

**BAKING METHOD:**

Place each turkey cutlet between two sheets of plastic wrap and pound with a meat mallet to ¼-inch thickness. Cut in half. Continue with remaining cutlets. Set aside. In a large skillet, heat 2 tbs. of the olive oil over medium-high heat. Stir in mushrooms, sprinkle with 1 tbs. of the garlic powder and cook for 4 minutes, until tender. Remove and set aside. Heat oven to 350°.

Coat a 9 x 13 x 2-inch oven-to-table pan with 1 tbs. of the olive oil. Sprinkle 5 or 6 of the cutlets with salt, pepper and garlic powder and dredge lightly in flour. Add 2 tbs. of the olive oil to skillet and sauté sprinkled cutlets for 6 minutes, turning once. Remove to prepared baking pan. Sprinkle with ⅓ of the reserved mushrooms. Repeat this procedure with remaining cutlets, adding more olive oil if needed. When all cutlets are cooked and layered with mushrooms in baking pan, pour Marsala wine into skillet over medium-high heat. Stir constantly to dislodge brown bits on bottom of pan. Add beef broth and bring to a boil. Boil for 1 minute to thicken slightly. Pour wine sauce over layered turkey and mushrooms. Place in oven and bake for 15 minutes, until bubbly and cooked through.

**NON-BAKING METHOD**

Sauté cutlets as described above, but do not layer in baking pan. When all cutlets are cooked, pour Marsala into skillet and cook over high heat for 2 minutes. Pour in beef stock and bring to a boil. Add reserved mushrooms and cutlets. Lower heat to a high simmer and cook, uncovered, until liquid reduces and becomes syrupy. Serve immediately on heated plates.

# GAME HENS WITH MUSHROOMS AND ARTICHOKES

*Served with herb-flavored rice, these game hens make an elegant dish, delicious with a pilaf and mixed green salad. Your butcher can split the game hens for you, and remove the backbones.*

4 Cornish game hens, cut in half with backbones removed
4 tsp. each dried sage and thyme
garlic powder
salt and freshly ground black pepper to taste
¼ cup extra virgin olive oil
2 pkg. (10 oz. each) frozen artichokes, thawed and quartered
½ lb. brown mushrooms, sliced
1 cup white wine
¼ cup balsamic vinegar
1 tbs. chicken stock base, or 1 chicken bouillon cube
1½ cups chicken broth
fresh sage leaves and lemon zest, for garnish

Rub each hen half with ½ tsp. each of the dried sage and thyme. Sprinkle liberally with garlic powder. Cover and refrigerate for at least 30 minutes.

Heat oven to 400°. Remove hens from refrigerator. Sprinkle each with ½ tsp. of the olive oil and season with salt and pepper. Place on a rack above a foil-lined baking sheet. Bake until plump and brown, about 30 minutes.

While hens are roasting, warm remaining 2½ tbs. olive oil in a large skillet over high heat. Sauté artichokes and mushrooms for 3 minutes, until lightly browned. Remove vegetables, cover and keep warm. Pour wine into skillet and reduce by half. Add vinegar, chicken stock base and chicken broth. Reduce by half. Stir in reserved vegetables and season with salt, pepper and remaining 1 tsp. sage. Divide vegetable sauté among 8 plates. Top with game hen pieces and garnish with sage leaves and lemon zest.

# CHICKEN WITH OLIVES AND SAFFRON

Servings: 4–6

*The North African influence on Southern Italian cooking is evident in this flavorful dish.*

salt and freshly ground black pepper
3 lb. chicken breasts, skin removed
3 large cloves garlic, smashed
1 tsp. finely chopped fresh ginger
grated zest of 1 lemon
½ tbs. capers, rinsed and drained
½ cup pitted, chopped green olives

½ tsp. powdered saffron
¼ cup extra virgin olive oil
1 can (14 oz.) chicken broth
1 cup water
1 tsp. honey
2 tbs. chopped fresh flat-leaf parsley
cooked, hot couscous

Salt and pepper chicken and set aside. In a food processor workbowl, pulse garlic, ginger, lemon zest, capers, olives and saffron until a coarse paste forms. In a large skillet, over medium-high heat, warm olive oil. Brown chicken for 15 minutes, turning once. Push chicken to sides of skillet. Add garlic-olive paste and cook until paste browns and becomes fragrant. Be careful not to burn. Stir in chicken broth and water. Bring to a boil. Rearrange chicken in pan. Lower heat, cover pan and simmer for 20 minutes, until chicken is cooked and sauce thickened. Transfer chicken to serving platter. Stir in honey and pour sauce over chicken pieces. Sprinkle with parsley and serve with couscous.

# FILLET OF SOLE WITH BASIL AND MINT

Servings: 4

*These fragrant herbs perk up the mild flavor of this popular fish while the white wine adds complexity. Choose a Pinot Grigio for best results. Any delicate white fish fillets will work in this recipe.*

2 lb. sole fillets
salt and freshly ground white pepper
flour for dusting
¼ cup extra virgin olive oil
⅓ cup thinly sliced shallots

1 cup chopped fresh basil leaves
¼ cup chopped fresh mint
1 cup white wine
½ cup chopped toasted almonds

Lightly salt, pepper and flour sole fillets. Set aside. In a large skillet, over medium-low heat, warm olive oil with shallots. Cook for 3 minutes, until soft and fragrant. Remove shallots from pan and set aside. Quickly sauté sole fillets in shallot oil for 2 minutes. Add basil, mint, wine and reserved shallots. Lower heat to a simmer. Loosen fillets from pan but continue to cook until wine has nearly evaporated. Divide fillets and herbal mixture among 4 serving plates. Top with almonds and serve immediately.

# CLAM FRITTERS WITH GARLIC MAYONNAISE

*Oven-frying these fritters produces a flavorful, golden brown crust without the added fat of conventional frying.*

2 cups packaged Italian seasoned breadcrumbs
2 tbs. chopped fresh flat-leaf parsley
2 tsp. dried oregano
2 cans (6½ oz. each) chopped clams with juice
1 egg, slightly beaten
¼ cup extra virgin olive oil

Heat oven to 500°. Line a baking sheet with 2 layers of foil. In the center of the top foil layer, mix breadcrumbs, parsley and oregano together. Form a well. Pour clams, juice and eggs in the well. With a fork, gradually mix breadcrumbs with clam mixture until moistened. If too dry, add water, 1 tbs. at a time. If too moist, add breadcrumbs until a firm but moist consistency is reached. Form into patties.

Remove top foil layer from baking sheet. Brush tops and bottoms of patties with olive oil and place on clean foil. Bake until golden brown and cooked through, about 8 minutes. Remove and serve with *Garlic Mayonnaise (Salsa di Aglio)*.

**GARLIC MAYONNAISE**　　　　Makes 1 cup
1 cup mayonnaise
1 tbs. garlic powder

In a serving dish, whisk together mayonnaise and garlic powder. Refrigerate, covered, until ready to use.

# MUSSELS IN WHITE WINE

*Cook shellfish in white wine rather than water for tenderness and flavor. Rinse mussels well before cooking to remove sand. Discard any mussels that do not open during cooking.*

4 cloves garlic, minced, divided
3 tbs. extra virgin olive oil, divided
8 slices Italian bread
1 cup chopped Roma (plum) tomatoes

1 cup crisp white wine
4½ lb. mussels, cleaned and de-bearded
3 sprigs fresh flat-leaf parsley, divided

Heat broiler. In a small bowl, mash together 2 cloves of the garlic with 2 tbs. of the olive oil. Spread mixture on 1 side of the bread slices. Place bread on baking sheet, garlic side up. Broil until golden, about 3 minutes. Set aside.

In a large skillet, over medium-high heat, warm remaining 1 tbs. olive oil. Add remaining 2 cloves garlic and tomatoes. Cook for 2 minutes until aromatic. Add wine. When bubbling, add mussels and 2 sprigs of the parsley. Cover and cook for 5 minutes, or until mussels open. Chop remaining 1 tbs. parsley. Serve mussels from skillet with cooking liquid, toasted bread and parsley.

86    POULTRY AND SEAFOOD

# BROILED OYSTERS

*Use this combination of breadcrumbs, olive oil, garlic and parsley on other shellfish for an easy preparation. Vary flavor by changing herbs and adding grated cheese.*

| | |
|---|---|
| 1 dozen oysters in the shell, shucked, or 2 jars fresh shucked oysters | 2 tsp. finely chopped fresh flat-leaf parsley |
| 1 cup breadcrumbs | ¼ cup extra virgin olive oil |
| 1 tsp. garlic powder | 2 lemons, cut into wedges, for garnish |

Heat broiler. If using fresh oysters in the shell, open oysters and use bottom shells as serving dishes. Arrange oysters in bottom shells on a foil-lined baking sheet. Otherwise, divide jarred oysters and liquor among 4 shallow baking dishes. In a small bowl, mix together breadcrumbs, garlic powder, parsley and olive oil, using just enough oil to moisten mixture. Spoon mixture over oysters. Broil until edges begin to curl and breadcrumb mixture is bubbly, about 5 minutes. Watch closely since breadcrumbs may burn.

Alternatively, oysters may be roasted in a 400° oven for 12 minutes. Serve with lemon wedges.

# SEA SCALLOPS WITH GRAPPA

*Today's grappa is a far cry from the harsh, potent brew of yesteryear distilled from the vintner's discarded grape skins and seeds.*

16 large sea scallops
salt and black pepper
1 tsp. sugar

¼ cup extra virgin olive oil, divided
¼ cup grappa, brandy or cognac
2 lemons, cut into wedges

Dry scallops thoroughly with paper towels. Season scallops with salt, pepper and a generous pinch of sugar. In a large skillet, over medium-high heat, warm 2 tbs. of the olive oil until shimmering. Increase heat, add first 8 scallops and sear quickly for 2 to 3 minutes on each side. Middle will be undercooked. Remove to serving dish and keep warm. Add remaining 2 tbs. olive oil, if necessary, and repeat procedure.

Remove scallops, pour in grappa, lower heat to medium and stir, scraping up caramelized bits with a wooden spoon. Cook until sauce reduces and thickens. Return scallops to skillet, coat with sauce and cook for 1 minute, until heated through. Pour back into serving dish and serve with lemon wedges.

# BAKED SALMON WITH ARTICHOKES

*This recipe takes minutes to assemble. Serve with a chilled Frascati.*

1 jar (4 oz.) marinated artichoke hearts, drained
1 lb. salmon fillets
¼ cup dry white wine
2 tbs. olive oil
salt

Heat oven to 350°. Process the artichoke hearts in a food processor workbowl for 10 seconds, until smooth. Place salmon fillets in 1 layer on foil-lined baking sheet. Spread artichoke puree over each salmon fillet. Pour wine around salmon, drizzle with olive oil and season with salt. Fold edges of foil to make an airtight package. Oven-poach salmon for 20 minutes. Remove from foil and serve with juices.

# VEGETABLES

Vegetables are the center of Italian cuisine. Cooked vegetables are used in combination with all other foods, alone, or as side dishes with meats, poultry and seafood. This section features vegetables as side dishes.

# SWEET AND SOUR PEPPERS

*The sweet and sour flavor combination, a favorite taste among the nobility of the Middle Ages, is enjoying popularity again. Balsamic vinegar, combined with raisins, sugar and high heat, transforms these simple broiled vegetables into a culinary delight.*

½ cup raisins
1 large green, yellow and red bell pepper, seeded and cut into ¼-inch strips
3 medium zucchini, cut into ¼-inch rounds
2 tbs. extra virgin olive oil

garlic powder to taste
salt and freshly ground pepper to taste
1 tbs. sugar
2 tbs. balsamic vinegar
¼ cup pine nuts, toasted

Cover raisins with hot water in a small bowl and steep for 10 minutes. Drain and set aside. Heat broiler. On a foil-lined baking sheet, mix peppers, zucchini, olive oil, garlic powder, salt and pepper. Broil for 12 minutes, stirring once. Add reserved raisins to pepper mixture. In a small bowl, whisk sugar into balsamic vinegar. Pour over vegetables and broil until liquid begins to caramelize, an additional 3 minutes. Spoon into serving dish and top with pine nuts.

# SNOW PEAS WITH PROSCIUTTO AND FENNEL

*Salty prosciutto is a savory foil to the sweetness of snow peas and fennel in this colorful dish.*

1½ lb. snow peas
3 tbs. extra virgin olive oil
2 oz. prosciutto, cut into small cubes
1 sprig fennel, chopped
1 tsp. anchovy paste
sea salt and freshly ground pepper

Bring a 4 quart stockpot of water to a boil over high heat. Remove tips and strings from snow peas. Blanch in boiling water for 1 minute. Immediately drain and run under cold water to stop cooking. Dry and set aside. In a large skillet, warm olive oil over medium-high heat. Sauté prosciutto for 2 minutes. Add fennel and anchovy paste. Stir until blended. Turn heat to high. Add reserved snow peas and cook for 2 to 3 minutes, until crisp-tender. Serve immediately or at room temperature.

# SWISS CHARD WITH GARBANZO BEANS

*Chard fresh from the garden or farmers' market, golden garbanzo beans and cherry tomatoes make a colorful, nutritious vegetable presentation.*

1 can (14 oz.) garbanzo beans, rinsed and drained
10 cups (1 large bunch) thinly sliced Swiss chard
garlic powder
10 cherry tomatoes, cut in half
¼ cup extra virgin olive oil
salt and freshly ground black pepper to taste
¼ cup grated Parmesan cheese

In a large, microwave-safe bowl, layer garbanzo beans with chard. Cover and microwave at full power for 3 minutes, or until cooked. Sprinkle with garlic powder to taste. Fold in cherry tomatoes and olive oil. Season with salt and pepper. Serve with Parmesan cheese.

# CORN ON THE COB WITH GORGONZOLA CHEESE

*Creamy Gorgonzola sauce adds richness to the corn.*

4 ears corn
3 oz. Gorgonzola cheese, crumbled
½ cup half-and-half
1 tbs. cognac

Wash corn and trim ends, but do not shuck. Place in the microwave oven and cook on full power until corn is tender. Set aside. In a small saucepan, over medium heat, whisk cheese with half-and-half. Cook until cheese is melted and sauce is smooth. Whisk in cognac. Keep warm. Shuck corn and serve with hot sauce.

# BROILED BUTTERNUT SQUASH AND KALE

Servings: 4

*The slightly smoky taste and texture of organic kale contrasts with the sweet, creamy texture of squash in this unusual vegetable presentation. Use organic or "Dino" kale for broiling since ordinary kale dries out under the intense heat.*

4 cups peeled and sliced butternut squash
1 tsp. chopped fresh rosemary
1 tsp. garlic powder
salt and freshly ground black pepper to taste
2 tbs. extra virgin olive oil, divided
4 cups thinly sliced organic kale

Heat broiler. Place squash, rosemary, garlic powder, salt and pepper and 1 tbs. of the oil in a large plastic bag. Shake bag to coat squash with oil and seasoning. Remove squash from bag and place on foil-lined baking sheet. Broil for 5 minutes. Place kale in the same bag and add remaining 1 tbs. oil, salt and pepper. Shake bag to coat kale, then add kale to partially cooked squash. Broil until squash is brown around edges and kale is smoky. Check seasonings and serve.

# ROASTED ASPARAGUS WITH TARRAGON AND WALNUTS

*No matter how it is prepared, the first asparagus of the season always tastes the best. Try this cooking method for a slightly chewy texture and a mild, herbal flavor.*

2½ lb. medium asparagus spears, tough ends removed
2 tbs. extra virgin olive oil
1 tsp. garlic powder
2 large sprigs fresh tarragon, chopped, or 1 tsp. dried
¼ cup chopped toasted walnuts

Heat oven to 500°. On a foil-lined baking sheet, toss asparagus with olive oil. Arrange in 1 layer. Sprinkle with garlic powder and tarragon. Roast for 8 to 10 minutes, until barely tender. Serve topped with walnuts.

# EGGPLANT WITH BASIL AND MINT

*Room temperature grilled or broiled vegetables are summertime treats — a treat for the cook, because they can be prepared ahead of time; and for the diners, for their incredible flavor!*

olive oil spray
1 large eggplant, cut into ½-inch-thick
   slices
garlic powder

¼ cup extra virgin olive oil
2 tbs. chopped fresh mint, or 2 tsp. dried
2 tbs. chopped fresh basil, or 2 tsp. dried
salt and freshly ground black pepper

Heat broiler. Coat a foil-lined baking sheet with olive oil spray. Arrange eggplant slices in batches in 1 layer. Sprinkle with garlic powder and spray with olive oil. Broil until light brown, about 8 minutes. Turn over, sprinkle with garlic powder, spray with olive oil, and broil until brown. Remove from pan and place in shallow serving bowl. Repeat process with remaining eggplant. Coat eggplant slices with olive oil, basil, mint, salt, pepper and additional garlic powder to taste. Serve at room temperature.

# GREEN BEANS WITH BALSAMIC MINT DRESSING

Servings: 4

*Mint and balsamic vinegar add a new flavor dimension to green beans. Make early in the day for a room-temperature vegetable accompaniment for grilled meats, poultry or seafood.*

½ lb. fresh green beans, ends removed
1 tbs. extra virgin olive oil
1 tsp. balsamic vinegar
1 tbs. chopped fresh mint, or 1 tsp. dried
salt and freshly ground pepper to taste

In a 4-quart saucepan, bring 6 cups water to a boil. Add green beans. Bring water to a second boil and cook beans for 3 to 5 minutes, until barely tender. Drain and plunge in ice water to stop cooking. In a serving bowl, whisk together oil, vinegar and mint. Drain beans, pat dry and fold into oil mixture. When beans are well coated with vinaigrette, cover and hold at room temperature until serving time. Season with salt and pepper before serving.

# MICROWAVE MUSHROOMS

*Quick, easy and delicious describes these mushrooms. Serve with grilled meats, stir into a sauce or use as a topping for pasta.*

1 lb. medium brown or white sliced mushrooms
1 tsp. hot red pepper flakes
1 tsp. garlic powder or more to taste
¼ cup finely chopped fresh parsley
¼ cup extra virgin olive oil
salt to taste

Arrange mushroom slices in 1 layer on a large microwave-safe platter. If platter is too small to hold all mushrooms, prepare in batches. Sprinkle with red pepper flakes, garlic powder and olive oil. Microwave on full power for 1 minute. Stir. Remove and cover until ready to serve.

# GARLIC POTATOES

*The natural mealiness of potatoes makes them a perfect vehicle for Italian flavors. The two recipes that follow are quick classics.* Roasted Rosemary Garlic Potatoes *compliment grilled foods, and* Triple Garlic Mashed Potatoes *are excellent with sauced foods.*

## ROASTED ROSEMARY GARLIC POTATOES

2 lb. small yellow, red or white potatoes
¼ cup extra virgin olive oil
4 tbs. chopped fresh rosemary
1 tsp. garlic powder
salt and freshly ground black pepper to taste

Heat oven to 450°. With a brush, scrub potatoes under running water. Dry. Put potatoes into a large plastic bag. Add olive oil, rosemary, garlic powder, salt and pepper. Hold bag closed and shake bag to coat potatoes with oil and seasoning. Pour onto a large, foil-lined baking sheet in a single layer. Bake for 40 minutes, or until potatoes are fork-tender. Serve with grilled or roasted foods.

**TRIPLE GARLIC MASHED POTATOES**

6 large baking potatoes, peeled and coarsely chopped
6 cloves garlic, crushed
2 tbs. roasted garlic-flavored olive oil
2 tbs. toasted freeze-dried garlic granules
salt and white pepper to taste

In a large saucepan over high heat, combine potatoes and garlic with water to cover. Bring to a boil. Lower heat, cover and simmer for 15 to 20 minutes, until potatoes and garlic are very soft. Drain, reserving 1 cup of the potato cooking water. In same pot, mash potatoes and garlic. Whisk in oil and enough reserved potato water to make potatoes creamy. Add salt and pepper. Spoon into a serving bowl and top with garlic granules. Keep warm in a 200° oven until ready to serve.

# ROASTED POTATOES, PEPPERS AND OLIVES

Servings: 4–6

*This colorful presentation is a contrast of textures and flavors—creamy, crispy, salty and sweet. Enjoy with grilled, baked and roasted entrées.*

4–6 large russet potatoes
3 large red bell peppers
3 tbs. extra virgin olive oil
3 cloves garlic, smashed

¼ cup fresh marjoram, or 1 tbs. dried
½ cup pitted kalamata olives
salt and freshly ground black pepper to
    taste

Heat oven to 450°. Peel potatoes, quarter and cut into ½-inch-thick slices. Put slices into a large locking plastic bag. Remove seeds and ribs from peppers and cut into chunks about the size of the potatoes. Place into bag with potatoes. Add oil, garlic and marjoram. Seal bag and shake to coat vegetables with oil mixture. Line a large baking sheet with foil. Arrange vegetable mixture in 1 layer, using a second sheet if necessary. Roast for 20 minutes, until almost cooked. Scatter olives over vegetables and cook for an additional 10 minutes. Season with salt and pepper.

# SALADS

Italians present salad as an entrée or as an ending to a meal. The entrée salad usually features cured meats, eggs, cooked rice, pasta, meats, poultry and/or seafood with greens, while the meal's-end salad is a basic leafy green salad with vegetables, herbs or fruit designed to aid digestion. Using purchased salad dressings is a timesaver for the busy cook. These dressings may also be used to flavor sauces or marinades. When time permits, make fresh vinaigrette dressings by using the classic 3 parts olive oil to 1 part vinegar or lemon juice. Expand on this theme by using flavored or aged vinegars such as herb, garlic, onion, raspberry, balsamic or sherry. Mustard and other condiments, fruit nectars and citrus zests also add variety to simple vinaigrettes.

# FENNEL SALAD

*There is a variety of tastes and textures in this innovative salad which comes together in record time, thanks to pre-washed, bagged greens and commercially prepared dressing.*

1 cup purchased white wine vinaigrette dressing
½ tsp. ground fennel seeds
8 cups mixed salad greens
2 tbs. chopped fresh mint
2 cups shaved fresh fennel, shaved with a vegetable peeler
1 cup pitted oil-cured black olives
1½ cups red seedless grapes
1 cup toasted walnuts
3 oz. firm sheep's milk or Parmesan cheese, shaved with a vegetable peeler
salt and freshly ground pepper

In a large salad bowl, whisk together vinaigrette and ground fennel seeds. Add salad greens, mint, fennel, olives, grapes, walnuts and cheese. Season with salt and pepper, toss and serve.

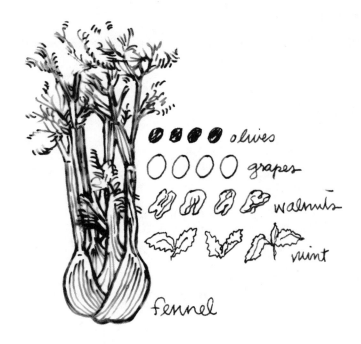

olives

grapes

walnuts

mint

fennel

# ESCAROLE WITH DRIED CRANBERRIES

*Raspberry vinaigrette mellows the sharpness of the escarole and tempers the sweetness of the cranberries. Serve with poultry entrées.*

3/4 cup purchased raspberry vinaigrette dressing
1/2 cup dried cranberries
8 cups torn escarole leaves
1/2 cup toasted hazelnuts, coarsely chopped
2 oz. Asiago or Parmesan cheese, shaved with a vegetable peeler
8 fresh mint leaves, thinly sliced

Pour raspberry vinaigrette into a large salad bowl. Add cranberries and escarole. Toss well. Top with hazelnuts, cheese and mint leaves. Serve immediately.

# WILTED SPINACH SALAD

*Prosciutto di Parma, balsamic vinegar and toasted pine nuts put the stamp of Italy on this easy-to-prepare salad.*

¼ lb. prosciutto, cut into strips
¼ cup extra virgin olive oil, divided
1½ tbs. balsamic vinegar
8–10 cups baby spinach leaves
1 cup shaved Parmesan cheese, shaved with a vegetable peeler
½ cup toasted pine nuts

In a large, microwave-safe bowl, combine prosciutto with 1 tbs. of the olive oil. Cook on high power for 30 seconds to crisp prosciutto. Mix in remaining 3 tbs. olive oil and balsamic vinegar. Gently fold in spinach, coating it with hot dressing. Sprinkle cheese shavings and pine nuts over top. Serve immediately.

# ENDIVE WITH ANCHOVY DRESSING

*This bright-tasting salad is a refreshing ending for a robust dinner.*

1 head endive
½ cup purchased anchovy vinaigrette dressing, or Caesar vinaigrette dressing
lemon juice to taste
salt and freshly ground pepper

Wash, dry and cut endive into bite-sized pieces. Toss with vinaigrette. Season with lemon juice, salt and pepper, and serve.

# SPINACH, PEAR AND GORGONZOLA SALAD

Servings: 6

*Mellow pears and spinach leaves pair well with Gorgonzola cheese. There is just enough tang in the raspberry vinegarette to cleanse the palate after a rich meal.*

½ cup purchased raspberry vinaigrette dressing
10 oz. baby spinach leaves
2 Bosc pears, cored and cut into chunks
½ cup toasted hazelnuts
½ cup crumbled Gorgonzola cheese

Place all ingredients in a large salad bowl. Mix well and serve.

# SICILIAN CITRUS SALAD

*This refreshing salad of navel oranges and sweet lemons is the perfect ending to a fish dinner. Look for sweet lemons in Middle Eastern markets. Meyer lemons or white grapefruit work well if sweet lemons are not available.*

12 escarole leaves, torn in large pieces
½ tsp. garlic powder
½ large fennel bulb, thinly sliced
4 navel oranges, peeled, seeded and thinly sliced crosswise
3 sweet lemons, peeled, seeded and thinly sliced crosswise
½ medium red onion, very thinly sliced
1 cup pitted oil-cured black olives
¼ cup chopped fresh mint leaves
extra virgin olive oil and lemon wedges, for garnish

Arrange escarole leaves on a large, flat serving platter. Sprinkle lightly with garlic powder. Spread fennel, orange and lemon slices over escarole. Top with onion slices, olives and mint. Serve with olive oil and lemon wedges.

# PIZZA, FRITTATA AND PANINI

Prepared dough makes pizza quick and easy. To ensure a crunchy, crisp crust, place a pizza stone or large quarry tile in a cold oven on the bottom rack: If you place the stone or tile in a hot oven, it will crack. Heat oven at 450° for at least 30 minutes before baking. Red wines such as Primativo or Zinfandel are great with pizza.

Frittata preparation is as simple as 1-2-3: **1.** Briefly sauté the "filler" in olive oil and cover with lightly beaten eggs. **2.** Cook until nearly set. **3.** Brown under the broiler.

Panini are Italian sandwiches usually made with chewy, flat loaves such as ciabatta or focaccia. These loaves are split and filled with simple combinations of preserved vegetables in olive oil, specialty cheeses, grilled or cold cured meats.

# PIZZA BIANCA WITH RED ONIONS

Makes one 12-inch pizza

*Caramelized red onions lend their sweetness to salty prosciutto and nutty Swiss cheese. To save prep time, the next time you bake potatoes, bake onions wrapped in foil at the same time. Temperature and baking time are the same for both.*

1 large red onion
1 tsp. olive oil
½ tsp. balsamic vinegar
1 lb. prepared pizza or bread dough
2 tbs. extra virgin olive oil
½ lb. thinly sliced prosciutto
1 cup grated Swiss cheese
salt and freshly ground black pepper

Place a pizza stone on the bottom rack of the oven and heat to 400°. Place peeled onion on a large square of foil. Drizzle with oil and vinegar and wrap onion tightly. Bake for about 45 minutes, or until very soft. Remove onion, unwrap and set aside. Raise oven temperature to 450°. Lightly oil a 12-inch pizza pan. Stretch dough with your fingertips to fit pan.

Alternatively, roll out to ½-inch thickness and place in pan. Brush dough with olive oil. Slice roasted onion and scatter over dough. Arrange prosciutto ribbons into "spokes" around pie. Top with cheese, salt and pepper. Bake until crust is golden and cheese is melted, about 12 to 15 minutes. Serve hot or warm.

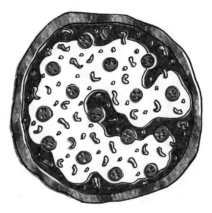

# PIZZA PUTTANESCA WITH CLAMS

Makes one 12-inch pizza

*The raw ingredients for Pasta Puttanesca enhance the flavor of the clams in this zesty pizza.*

1 lb. prepared pizza dough
2 tbs. extra virgin olive oil, divided
8–10 cherry tomatoes, cut in half
1 can (10 oz.) clams, drained
1 tbs. capers, rinsed and drained
1 can (2 oz.) anchovies, coarsely chopped
1 tsp. hot red pepper flakes
¼ cup grated pecorino romano cheese

Place pizza stone on the lowest rack and heat the oven to 450°. Lightly brush pan with 1 tbs. of the oil. With fingers, stretch dough to fit pan and brush with 1 tbs. of the oil. Arrange tomatoes, clams, capers and anchovies on dough; sprinkle with pepper flakes and cheese. Drizzle remaining 1 tbs. of oil over top of pizza. Bake until edges are golden brown and center is bubbly, about 15 minutes. Serve hot or warm.

# CALZONE WITH RED PEPPER

*Rosemary bread dough is the base for this "fold-over-pizza" whose name means "pantaloons" in Italian. Briefly knead chopped rosemary into plain dough if you can't find prepared rosemary dough. Use commercially prepared artichokes, peppers and garlic to save time.*

1 lb. rosemary bread dough
3 tbs. garlic-flavored olive oil
½ cup marinated artichokes, chopped
½ cup roasted red peppers, chopped
1 tbs. roasted garlic, chopped

¼ cup mozzarella cheese, coarsely grated
1 egg, slightly beaten
1 tbs. chopped fresh rosemary, or 1 tsp.
  dried

Place pizza stone on lowest rack and heat oven to 450°. Lightly brush pan with 1 tbs. of the oil. With fingers, stretch dough to fit pan and brush with 1 tbs. of the oil. Leaving a 1-inch border, arrange artichokes, peppers and roasted garlic on ½ of the pie. Top with mozzarella cheese. Drizzle with remaining 1 tbs. oil. Paint edge of pie with egg. Carefully fold dough over, press down on edge and seal with fork tines. Brush remaining egg over top of calzone and sprinkle with rosemary. Bake until top is golden brown and crisp, about 15 minutes. Serve warm or cold.

# PIZZA PINWHEELS WITH ANCHOVIES
# AND RED PEPPER FLAKES

*This pizza has its roots in Calabria. It is a favorite New Year's Eve snack, served with a lusty red wine before midnight. In Italy, the day before a feast day was always meatless, hence the anchovies.*

1 lb. prepared pizza dough
2 cans (2 oz. each) anchovy fillets in olive oil, chopped, oil reserved
4 cloves garlic, minced
2 tbs. hot red pepper flakes
1 tsp. dried oregano

Place pizza stone on the bottom rack and heat the oven to 450°. Lightly oil a baking sheet and set aside. Roll dough into a ¼-inch-thick rectangle, about 6 x 15 inches in size. In a small bowl, mix together anchovies, oil, garlic and red pepper flakes. Spread mixture thinly over dough. It will not cover completely. Sprinkle with oregano. Starting with a long side, roll dough up jelly-roll style. Turn seam down. Cut into 1-inch slices and place on a prepared baking sheet. Bake until golden brown, about 12 to 15 minutes. Serve warm or cold.

# ARTICHOKE FRITTATA

*Frittatas make a nourishing accompaniment to soups. Try this one with* Butternut Squash and Kale Soup, *page 24.*

1 tbs. extra virgin olive oil
1 cup chopped green onions
1 cup marinated artichoke hearts, drained and chopped
2 tbs. minced fresh marjoram or parsley
5 eggs

2 tbs. milk
1 cup grated pecorino romano cheese, divided
salt and freshly ground black pepper to taste

Heat broiler. In a bowl, lightly beat eggs with milk and ½ cup of the cheese; set aside. In a medium skillet with a heat-resistant handle, warm olive oil over medium heat. Sauté green onions for 3 minutes, until wilted. Add artichoke hearts and marjoram and briefly sauté. Pour egg mixture over artichoke mixture and cook until edges are set but top is still moist. Sprinkle top of frittata with remaining ½ cup cheese and place under broiler until golden brown. Cut into 4 portions and serve immediately.

# ZUCCHINI, PEPPER AND MUSHROOM FRITTATA

Servings: 2

*Broiled vegetables are the base of this quick supper for two. The recipe can be doubled, but use two skillets for faster cooking. Frascati, a slightly "fizzy" white wine from Rome compliments the frittata.*

3 tbs. extra virgin olive oil, divided
1 zucchini, sliced into ¼-inch coins
½ red bell pepper, sliced ¼-inch thick
½ cup sliced green onions
4 brown mushrooms, thinly sliced

3 eggs, slightly beaten
salt and freshly ground black pepper
3 tbs. coarsely grated provolone cheese
1 tbs. finely chopped fresh flat-leaf parsley

Heat broiler. On a foil-lined baking sheet, toss zucchini, pepper, onions and mushrooms with 1 tbs. of the olive oil. Broil until almost tender, about 5 minutes; leave broiler on. Warm remaining 2 tbs. olive oil in an 8-inch skillet, over medium heat. Scrape broiled vegetables into skillet and pour eggs over. Season with salt and pepper. Cook over medium heat for 3 minutes, until edges are set but center is still moist. Remove from heat. Sprinkle with cheese and parsley. Place under broiler until cheese melts and frittata is golden. Serve immediately.

# PANINI GRECALE

*This sandwich comes from Restorante Bouga Bouga in Porto Cervo, Sardinia, where panini are named after the local winds. The scirocco comes from North Africa; the Grecale from Greece! If you can't find sweet Gorgonzola you can use regular Gorgonzola and mix it with some butter.*

4 ciabatta panini rolls
2 oz. Gorgonzola dolce, or 1½ oz. Gorgonzola
    mashed with 1 tbs. soft butter
¼ lb. Mortadella, sliced paper-thin

Split and lightly toast panini rolls in toaster or oven. Spread both sides of each roll with Gorgonzola. Add 2 slices mortadella. Close and lightly press together.

Panini

# GRILLED VEGETABLE PANINI

*This is a great vegetarian sandwich for summer parties and barbecues. Use commercially prepared vegetables in oil.*

1 loaf ciabatta, focaccia or any crusty bread
4 tbs. porcini mushroom spread, or ½ cup minced mushrooms sautéed with 1 tsp. butter
4 grilled eggplant slices in oil
4 red pepper slices in oil
4 marinated artichoke hearts
extra virgin olive oil
salt and freshly ground black pepper

Heat oven to 200°. Warm ciabatta bread in oven. Cut loaf into 4 large pieces and split each section in half. Spread with porcini mushroom spread. Arrange 1 slice each of eggplant, red pepper and artichoke on bottom half of each sandwich. Drizzle with olive oil and season with salt and pepper. Cover with top section of bread and warm in a 200° oven for 10 minutes.

# PANINI CAPRESE

*"Caprese" simply means, "from the island of Capri"! Think of this panini as a portable Caprese salad, the classic presentation of sliced tomatoes, mozzarella and fresh basil.*

4 Italian panini rolls, or use focaccia or any crusty bread
1/2 cup pesto
2 beefsteak tomatoes
1 large buffalo mozzarella, cut into 8 slices
olive oil
salt

Cut rolls and spread each generously with pesto. Place two slices of tomato and two slices buffalo mozzarella on each roll. Drizzle with olive oil, season with salt and serve.

PIZZA, FRITTATA AND PANINI    121

# GRILLED CHICKEN PANINI WITH FONTINA CHEESE

Servings: 4

*For a quick summer meal, serve this elegant panini with chilled soup.*

8 large slices sourdough bread, lightly toasted
1 container (8 oz.) mushroom pesto
2 cups baby arugula leaves
2 grilled chicken breast halves, sliced thin
2 oz. fontina cheese, shaved
olive oil spray

Place bread slices on work area. Spread bread with pesto. Place arugula leaves over pesto. On four of the prepared bread slices, layer chicken slices with cheese shavings. Cover with remaining bread slices. Press down lightly. Spray both sides of panini with olive oil. Preheat indoor grill, sandwich maker or panini press for 5 minutes. Working in batches, grill panini for 3 minutes, until cheese melts and pesto soaks into bread.

# DOLCI (DESSERTS)

In Italy, sweets are eaten either mid-morning or mid-afternoon rather than at the end of a meal. Taking time to relax over an espresso and a rich sweet is part of "la dolce vita" that we Americans so enjoy when in Italy. Bring the sweetness of Italy into your home. Below are some quick treats to be served anytime.

# GELATO PRONTO

Makes 8 half-cup servings

*Gelato is rich, dense Italian ice cream. Select a high-quality natural ice cream for this exotic Sicilian treat. Look for flower waters in Middle Eastern grocery stores.*

1 qt. natural vanilla ice cream
3 tbs. rose or orange flower water

Early in the day, soften ice cream for about 10 minutes in the refrigerator. Spoon ice cream into a large bowl. Stir in rose flower water. Blend quickly, return to container and re-freeze. Serve with purchased pizzelle cookies or biscotti at midday or after dinner. For a summer breakfast treat, enclose in a warm brioche or croissant and enjoy with an espresso or cappuccino.

## VARIATIONS

Mix flavored Italian syrups, such as Torani, with natural vanilla or chocolate ice cream for an endless variety of taste combinations. Start with 1 tbs. syrup and add to taste, since these syrups are more concentrated than flower waters.

# LIQUEUR PUDDING WITH PISTACHIOS

*Dessert wines adds richness to puddings and cakes. For a more intense pistachio flavor, use instant pistachio pudding.*

1 cup shelled pistachio nuts
$3/4$ cup Moscato wine, sweet vermouth or cream sherry
1 cup cold milk
2 tbs. orange flower water, optional
1 pkg. instant vanilla pudding mix

Heat oven to 400°. On a foil-lined baking sheet, spread nuts and toast for about 10 minutes. Cool. In a 4-cup glass pitcher or bowl, pour wine, milk and flower water. Stir. Add pudding mix. Whisk for 2 minutes, until smooth. Fold in all but 12 of the pistachio nuts. Pour pudding into 4 dessert dishes. Garnish with remaining nuts. Chill until serving time. This recipe may be doubled.

# TIRAMISU

*Tiramisu means "pick me up" in Italian. When spirits are down this heavenly dessert will set things right again. Be aware that dishes prepared with raw eggs can pose a health risk.*

6 very fresh eggs, separated
1 lb. mascarpone cheese, room
    temperature
½ cup Frangelico, or other hazelnut-
    flavored liqueur, divided

½ cup sugar
1½ cups warm espresso
one 7 oz. pkg. ladyfingers (24 pieces)
unsweetened cocoa powder

In a small bowl, with an electric mixer, whip egg whites until stiff peaks form. Set aside. Wash and dry beaters. In a large bowl, beat egg yolks until frothy. Add mascarpone, 6 tbs. of the Frangelico and sugar. Continue beating until thick and creamy. Gently fold reserved whites into yolk mixture until combined. In a shallow bowl, mix remaining 2 tbs. Frangelico with espresso. Quickly dip 1 side of each ladyfinger in espresso mixture. Holding dry side down, line the bottom and sides of an 8 x 11-inch glass dish. Spoon mascarpone mixture over soaked ladyfingers and smooth top. Cover with plastic wrap and chill for 1 or 2 hours. When ready to serve, sprinkle top with unsweetened cocoa powder.

# CHOCOLATE AMARETTO CAKE

*This elegant cake rivals those created in a fine pasticceria. To double the pleasure, serve with freshly brewed espresso and tiny glasses of amaretto.*

1 chocolate fudge cake mix for a 2-layer cake
3 eggs, room temperature
1 cup water
½ cup amaretto liqueur, divided
½ cup olive or canola oil
¾ cup confectioners' sugar
½ cup toasted almonds, cut into slivers

Heat oven to 350°. Oil a 10-cup bundt pan. In a large bowl, combine cake mix, eggs, water, ⅓ cup of the amaretto and oil. Beat at low speed for about 2 minutes, until all ingredients are blended. Pour into pan and bake until cake tests done, about 35 to 45 minutes. Cool and invert onto a serving platter. In a small bowl, whisk confectioners' sugar and remaining amaretto until thick and creamy. Drizzle mixture with a whisk over top of cake so it runs down the sides. Sprinkle nuts over top.

# TORTA DI RICOTTA

*A Sicilian cheesecake is the best description of this special dessert. Pour Marsala and delight your guests!*

2 cups biscotti crumbs
3 tbs. olive oil
4 tbs. Marsala wine, divided
2 eggs, well beaten
½ cup sugar
2 tbs. orange flower water

15 oz. ricotta cheese
½ cup confectioners' sugar
2 oz. mini chocolate chips
2 oz. candied orange and lemon zest,
    finely chopped
grated zest of 1 lemon and 1 orange

Heat oven to 350°. Butter bottom and sides of an 8-inch springform pan. In a small bowl, mix biscotti crumbs, olive oil and 3 tbs. of the Marsala. Mixture will just hold together. If too dry, add more wine. Using a spatula, press mixture into pan and up sides. Bake until set, about 15 minutes. Remove from oven and set aside. In a large bowl, combine eggs, sugar, orange flower water and remaining Marsala. Beat until frothy. Beat in ricotta, alternating with confectioners' sugar. Fold in chocolate chips, candied fruit and lemon and orange zests. Pour into reserved crust. Smooth top with spatula and bake for 1½ hours, until set. Refrigerate until cold.

# FRESH PEACHES IN PROSECCO

*If one could improve on the flavor of a freshly picked peach, this would be the way. Choose perfectly ripe peaches for the best flavor.*

4 peaches, peeled and sliced into wedges
1 bottle Prosecco or sparkling wine
8 large fresh mint leaves for garnish

Arrange several wedges of peaches in 8 martini glasses or dessert bowls. Cover with Prosecco. Garnish with mint leaves. Serve immediately.

# ALMOND MILK

Servings: 4

*Use organic marzipan, a candy paste made from ground almonds and sugar, for this refreshing Sicilian drink.*

2 tbs. marzipan
2 cups water
cracked ice cubes

Place marzipan in blender. Add water and blend until smooth. Pour over ice. Serve.

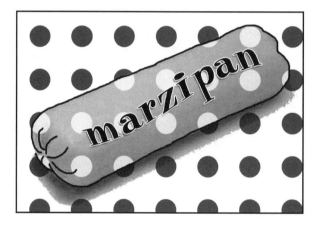

# MAKE-AHEAD RECIPES

Despite the abundance of convenience foods for "shortcut" cooking, sometimes it is worthwhile to produce these staples in advance and refrigerate or freeze to use as needed. The obvious advantages are superior taste, purer ingredients and lower cost.

# SOFFRITO

*This is the main flavor base for soups, stews, sauces and risotto.*

2 large yellow onions, coarsely chopped
2 large carrots
2 stalks celery
1/4 cup extra virgin olive oil

In a food processor workbowl, working in batches, finely chop onions, carrots and celery. Transfer to a large bowl as needed. In a very large skillet, over medium heat, warm olive oil. Add chopped vegetables and increase heat. Stirring constantly, cook for 8 to 10 minutes, until vegetables are soft and fragrant. If vegetables are cooking too quickly, lower heat, since vegetables should not brown. Pour back into large bowl and cool. When cool, place in 1-cup quantities in 1-quart freezer bags. Flatten bag and freeze. Each bag contains enough soffrito for most recipes.

# PESTO

*Authentic pesto is made with a mortar and pestle, but it is very time-consuming. Try making pesto in a blender or food processor for a faster result.*

4 packed cups fresh basil leaves, washed and dried
3 cloves garlic, coarsely chopped
¼ cup toasted pine nuts
1 cup olive oil
½ cup finely grated Parmesan cheese
¼ tsp. salt

Make sure basil leaves are completely dry. Place them in a blender with garlic and pine nuts and pulse until finely chopped. Add olive oil, cheese and salt. Blend until smooth. Use with pasta, grilled foods, panini, and as a flavor booster for soups and stews. Freeze leftover pesto in ice cube trays. Pop out frozen cubes and store in freezer bags.

# FAST TOMATO SAUCE

Makes 2 cups

*You can use this sauce on pizza if you substitute oregano for basil and puree it in a blender. Or serve over cooked pasta with grated Parmesan or romano cheese.*

2 pounds fresh tomatoes
¼ cup extra virgin olive oil
4 garlic cloves, sliced
6 fresh basil leaves, torn
salt to taste

Cut tomatoes into chunks. In a large skillet, heat oil over medium heat. Add garlic and sauté for 1 minute, until golden. Remove garlic and discard. Add tomatoes, basil and salt. Bring to a boil, reduce heat to medium and simmer for about 25 minutes, or until sauce has a thick and chunky consistency.

# ONE-HOUR RICH TOMATO SAUCE

Makes 4 quarts

*When marinara sauce is too light, dress more hearty pasta dishes with this rich tomato-herb sauce. For a heart-healthy entree add* Turkey Meatballs, *page 136, to the sauce 30 minutes before sauce is finished.*

3 tbs. extra virgin olive oil
4 cloves garlic, minced
1 tsp. spicy red pepper flakes
1 can (28 oz.) tomato puree
3 cups water
½ cup tomato paste
1 tsp. fennel seeds

½ tsp. allspice
1 tbs. dried oregano
1 bay leaf
6 fresh basil leaves, thinly sliced
salt and freshly ground black pepper to
    taste

In a 6-quart saucepan, warm olive oil over medium-high heat. Sauté garlic and red pepper for 1 minute. Add tomato puree, water, tomato paste, fennel, allspice, oregano and bay leaf. Bring to a boil. Lower heat and simmer, uncovered, for 30 minutes. If using turkey meatballs, add meatballs to sauce along with basil. Cook for an additional 30 minutes, until sauce is thick and very aromatic.

# TURKEY MEATBALLS

*Ground turkey makes a good substitute for the traditional meats in meatballs. The flavor is the same, but the texture is softer than the more sturdy beef, veal and pork.*

2 lb. ground turkey
2 cups seasoned Italian breadcrumbs
1 cup grated Parmesan cheese
1 tbs. dried oregano
2 tsp. garlic powder

¼ cup chopped fresh flat-leaf parsley
salt and freshly ground black pepper to
   taste
2 eggs
olive oil spray

Heat broiler. In a large bowl, mix together turkey, breadcrumbs, cheese, oregano, garlic powder, parsley, salt and pepper. Add eggs and mix with a wooden spoon until ingredients are well blended. Shape into 2-inch meatballs and place on a foil-lined baking sheet. Lightly spray meatballs with olive oil. Broil until golden, about 6 minutes. Turn over and spray with olive oil. Broil an additional 6 minutes.

# BREAD MACHINE PIZZA DOUGH
Makes 2 thin 12-inch crusts or 1 thick 12-inch

*Use your bread machine to make pizza dough.*

1 cup water
1 tsp. salt
2½ cups unbleached flour

1 cup cake flour
1½ tsp. active dry yeast

In the kneading pan of the bread machine, pour in water and spoon in salt, flours and yeast. Set machine to the dough cycle and start process. Dough should be ready to roll or press into pans in 2 hours.

# BREADCRUMBS

Collect stale, dry Italian or French bread slices from your table. Store them in paper bags. Working in batches, put bread into a locking plastic bag, coarsely crush with a meat mallet, process with a blender or food processor workbowl to desired consistency, pour into glass jars and refrigerate. Unflavored crumbs keep indefinitely.

# INDEX

## Serve Creative, Easy, Nutritious Meals with nitty gritty® Cookbooks

**For a free catalog, call:  Bristol Publishing Enterprises**
**(800) 346-4889**
**www.bristolpublishing.com**